STORE PRESENTATION & DESIGN No.4

STORE PRESENTATION & DESIGN No.4

Martin M. Pegler

RSD Publishing, Inc.
302 Fifth Avenue, New York, NY

RSD Publishing, Inc.
302 Fifth Avenue
New York, NY 10001
212-279-7004
CS@rsdpublishing.com
www.rsdpublishing.com

Distributors to the trade in the United States and Canada
Innovative Logistics
575 Prospect Street
Lakewood NJ 08701
732-363-5679

Distributors outside the United States and Canada
HarperCollins International
10 East 53rd Street
New York, NY 10022-5299

Library of Congress Cataloging in Publication Data:
Store Presentation and Design No. 4

Printed and Bound in Hong Kong
ISBN: 978-0-9826128-5-9

TABLE OF CONTENTS

INTRODUCTION **ICEBERG**

What is Visual Merchandising? It is a question that seems to have different meanings to different people and yet is a universal expression. When I lecture in foreign lands where English is not the first language, and I am being translated into the native tongue, I always hear "visual merchandise" stuck in amid all the foreign words. On page 218 in this edition, we asked architects, store designers, visual merchandisers and display people to define the expression. And as you will see, each sees it from a different angle, another view, and yet all agree that visual merchandising is important.

Since I have been around in this field for decades and witnessed the numerous changes that have occurred in the retail design industry, I would like to add my definition as well. Many years ago I heard a speaker say something that I have since adopted as my own and often refer to in my own lectures. It is the comparison of the retail store to an iceberg. The "Titanic" reasoning goes like this.

Every good and successful retail operation has to have a firm and solid base which keeps it secure and anchored in the shifting tides of the economy. That base consists of the retailer's business acumen — knowledge of the field — knowledge of the suppliers — the target market and his or her ability to buy the best products at the best price — and then sell them at the fairest prices. Retailers must know how to establish themselves in the community — in the market — be able to tie-in with the shoppers and have the kind of service and service-providers that help to make a store's reputation. It means trained sales people, good relations with the shoppers and a continued relationship with the customer after the sale has been made.

But, all of these factors necessary to the store's success lie beneath the waterline and are not visible to the shopper. What the shopper sees is what rises up above the waterline. Some — who don't know better — say that it just so much decoration and frou-frou. However, what the shopper actually sees and what makes the first and often most lasting impression of that store is based on the design, the decor and the ambiance of the retail space.

The store's windows are the official greeters and they are part of the tip of the iceberg. They make the first impression. They not only show the range and quality of the merchandise within but, by the manner in which the merchandise is shown, they create the store's look — image — appeal. The windows should reach out and envelop the shopper and draw him or her in. They should show some sense of class and style and indicate the type of shopper who would want to shop here. Once inside the store that first impression is either reinforced and solidified — or it all sinks.

The temperature in the store matters! The light levels and how the light is distributed matters. The kind of light that is used matters. The color and general overall tone of the space matters. The true test comes when shoppers go looking for what they came in for. Is there a helpful person there to assist? Are there clear and understandable signs? Directionals? Graphics that show and help to sell? Visual aids and displays? How does the shopper know where anything is?

Once shoppers find the line-up of products or garments they sought — how do they know which is which and what goes with what? Are there lifestyle vignettes with mannequins arranged to show how the garments can be mixed and matched? Are there eye-tempting displays that "show & sell"? Are there colored graphics that show the "look"? Are items brought together from all over the store to create an attractive, impulse-shopping experience? Are we providing a store filled with "ohs" and "ahs" and "I must have" products? This is where the shopper makes her buying decision.

Maybe it is all sugar coating and pink icing on this tip of the iceberg but it is what the shoppers see — what excites them — stimulates them and makes them want to buy. All of this "eye-candy" is the visual merchandising and display that makes it easier for the shopper to see — to select — to put together — and to buy. AND YES! Good salesmanship, knowledgeable help, welcoming and courteous behavior are also a visible part of the retail iceberg tip. It is here that the company's policies and purchasing acumen are tested and proven.

This book contains a "tip of the iceberg" selection of outstanding stores where the store architecture, the visual merchandising and displays excel. Whether it is an upmarket department store or boutique, or a high street specialty store or an outlet for a mass marketer, the trinity is working to create the brand image — and sell the product.

So, no floating vests or lifeboats will be necessary on this smooth voyage. Enjoy your tour around these "icebergs" that are not only a pleasure to see up close, but an education in retailing as well.

Martin M. Pegler

Podium

Jeddah, Saudi Arabia

DESIGN
Umdasch Shop Concept, Dubai, UAE

FIXTURES & PHOTOGRAPHY
Umdasch, Amstetten, Austria

There seems to always be something new and different coming up in the Middle East and this time it is the sprawling 35,000 sq. meter Podium Department Store in the Red Sea Mall in Jeddah. As planned and executed by Umdasch Shop Concept, "It offers modern, timeless design of the highest international level with a hint of One Thousand and One nights." Umdasch placed great emphasis on "achieving a successful balance between casual flair and elegance."

This new store also is a careful and successful balance between "modern international design" and the local "taste" of the discriminating Arab clientele. That "balance" is also seen in the material palette selected by the designers. There are high grade woods and exquisite, costly stone floors and these are juxtaposed with retro elements and polyester. Tying it all together are the Umdasch shop-fitting systems that not only add to the visual ambiance of the assorted departments, but also were designed to "permit a flexible and professional product presentation." Since SERVICE — spelled in capital letters — is a vital element in any store in this region of the world — and especially with such a sophisticated and demanding clientele, a V.I.P. lounge was created in the center of the store where clients can receive the sort of one-on-one service and guidance they have come to expect.

The overall feeling is light, bright and open. The almost pearly white/ beige palette is accentuated with highlights of color that often designate where the shopper is. Geometric patterns and shapes are used as decorative motifs since Podium is in Saudi

Arabia, a Muslim country, and thus there are no life-style graphics or any images of humans used in the directionals or the decorations. The brands that are featured in this store include Dior, Dolce y Gabbana, and Armani as well as noted casual brands such as Nike, addidas and Levi's. All have been selected to attract a truly discriminating clientele. Children's collections by famous designers are much in demand in Saudi Arabia and thus they appear prominently in the children's departments.

The customer friendly store layout and the profes-

sional visual merchandising distinguish this Al Garawi Group's store in Jeddah where Umdasch displayed the full range of services — "from store branding to realization."

For decades the Al Garawi Group, a family of Arab retailers, have been the leading shoe and leather goods retailers in the Middle East. With the inauguration of their Podium Department Store in the Red Sea Mall in Jeddah, and the opportunity to establish the Podium shop brand—most of the street level of the spacious store is devoted to numerous shops-

within-the-shop where shoes and handbags are presented. The presentation or visual merchandising of the different brands and the various levels of exclusivity of the designer lines are all distinguished by the numerous fixtures and fittings created by the Umdasch shop fitting division.

There are large open areas with numerous shoes on display—by category and by gender—and then there are the "boutiques" — the small, precious spaces with a few bags or shoes artfully arranged almost like artwork in a gallery. In the various shoe areas the seating is appropriate to the "class" of the product. In the women's area there are large framed mirrors and wide frames around the wall mounted shelves—finished in a dull gold — to complement the white/ beige walls and the marble floors. Then there are the sweeping curves, the arced fixtures and the bowed displayers. In contrast, in the men's departments the natural wood fixtures and the straight lines of the rear walls are marked off into display cubicles where the featured shoes are presented.

Shown on these pages are some of the numerous shoe and handbag areas as they are merchandised and presented in the new Podium store.

House of Fraser

Belfast, Northern Ireland

DESIGN
Kinnersley Kent Design, London, UK

PHOTOGRAPHER
Peter Cook

The recently opened 200,000 sq. ft. House of Fraser is located at the heart of the Victoria Square development in Belfast in Northern Ireland. This upscale fashion department store is already well known throughout the UK with its several bright and contemporary stores many of which have also been designed by Kinnersley Kent Design of London. This new store features over 500 fashion and lifestyle brands over the five levels of the store and as many as 150 brands are being introduced to this area for the first time.

Already the store is a "recognizable landmark on the Belfast skyline" with its soaring glass dome that tops the building's curved façade. The glass, look-through façade "previews the entrances to all the store's floors to create a striking backdrop to the dome" which is an attraction. Visitors may ascend 25 meters to get breathtaking panoramic views of the city.

The store has two levels of underground parking and on the lower ground floor the designers have introduced not only beauty and fashion accessories but a new concept for women's shoes. An exclusive Champagne & Oyster Bar is also located on this level and is destined to be

the "in" luncheon meeting place for fashionable citizens of Belfast. Many of the new men's wear labels can be viewed in the men's wear department which has been set on the upper ground level of House of Fraser. Sharing this floor is a new luggage department and the first Caffe Nero in Belfast.

Women's wear, lingerie and evening wear are on the first floor and along with the previously mentioned men's wear — these "fashion floors" serve not only to showcase well-known brands but introduce "new, exciting Irish talent." "The feel and mood of the men's and women's departments is sophisticated and exciting."

The second floor is devoted to an extensive home collection as well as a children's wear department that features Hamley's, the famous Regent St. of London toy store. This is their first exposure to Northern Ireland. Throughout, the designers, in conjunction with the client, gave "stronger floor-to-ceiling presence and scale to the concessions' areas to maximize their brand impact." "Ba Mizu," a bar and restaurant with an outdoor terrace with a fabulous view, is on the

top floor and is also a vibrant addition to Belfast's night life. It has its own elevator so that guests can arrive and depart after the store's closing hours.

Paul McElroy, partner at Kinnersley Kent, said, "The design of the Belfast store brings together the sleek sophistication that KKD has made the signature of the House of Fraser. The investment in design reflects House of Fraser's vision of becoming the U.K. and Ireland's leading department store for designer brands and premium shopping experiences." The Chief Executive of H of F, John King, added, "Our new store not only reflects this in terms of design and architecture, but also in the line-up of brands and experiences which we are introducing to the city and the region." The "this" in the last sentence refers to a truly world class shopping experience in Belfast.

Neiman Marcus

Lenox Square Mall, Atlanta, GA

DESIGN
Charles Sparks & Co., Westchester, IL

PRESIDENT & CEO
Charles Sparks

EXEC. VP & ACCOUNT EXECUTIVE
Don Stone

CREATIVE DIRECTOR
David Koe

ACCOUNT COORDINATOR:
Stephen Prosser

DIRECTOR RESOURCE STUDIO
Rachel Mikolajczyk

ARCHITECT
**SJW Architects & Associates,
Stan Weisbrod,** Westchester, IL

PHOTOGRAPHY
Charlie Mayer, Oak Park, IL
www.charlie_mayer.com

Neiman Marcus's Team

SENIOR VP
Wayne Hussey

VP PROPERTIES DEVELOPMENT
Cliff Suen

VP VISUAL PLANNING & STORE DEVELOPMENT
Ignaz Gorischek

SR. PROJECT MANAGER:
Victor Molaschi

DIRECTOR OF STORE PLANNING
Chris Lebamoff

DESIGNER
Megan Theriot

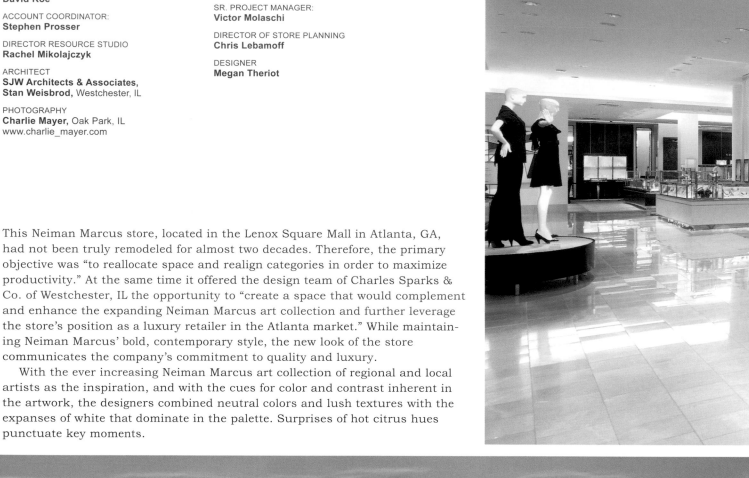

This Neiman Marcus store, located in the Lenox Square Mall in Atlanta, GA, had not been truly remodeled for almost two decades. Therefore, the primary objective was "to reallocate space and realign categories in order to maximize productivity." At the same time it offered the design team of Charles Sparks & Co. of Westchester, IL the opportunity to "create a space that would complement and enhance the expanding Neiman Marcus art collection and further leverage the store's position as a luxury retailer in the Atlanta market." While maintaining Neiman Marcus' bold, contemporary style, the new look of the store communicates the company's commitment to quality and luxury.

With the ever increasing Neiman Marcus art collection of regional and local artists as the inspiration, and with the cues for color and contrast inherent in the artwork, the designers combined neutral colors and lush textures with the expanses of white that dominate in the palette. Surprises of hot citrus hues punctuate key moments.

23

Among the newly created spaces is the designer jewelry department. Here the Charles Sparks team introduced a new vitrine or showcase concept for Atlanta: slick glass cubes with textured hammered glass backs suspended in floor to ceiling dividers. The showcases are set at multiple heights "to create a more animated visual horizon." The David Yurman jewelry shop is framed in by large circular showcase tables and set adjacent to the floor to ceiling windows along the back wall.

According to the design team: "The store was planned for ease of navigation and designed using attractors to move shoppers between areas. The concept terminology developed to describe these places of emphasis was 'moments of luxury.' The overall design challenge was to create a contemporary, but not hard edge environment; one that is comfortably modern."

Artisan lighting was introduced in several areas such as the twisted hand-crafted glass ribbons that are suspended in a large central concentric in the intimate apparel department. "Hundreds of ribbons cast a shimmering light in the space." A circular plate of stainless steel pierced with colorful glass pendant lights in sherbet colors highlights the bar seating area in the NM Café. Bold reveals break up the expansive ceilings in contemporary sportswear and contain adjustable track lights. "The reveals meet walls transferring this dramatic break-up to the perimeter."

The designers combined disciplines of architecture, interior design, and lighting to promote the luxury concept for this store. "Neiman Marcus has always demonstrated a unique connection to the communities it serves. While offering the best, this retailer recognizes the importance of the transformational shopping experience that goes beyond the traditional boundaries of retailing." A visit to this art-filled emporium of noted brand name and designer merchandise makes for an enriching experience.

Parkson

Kuala Lumpur, Malaysia

DESIGN
Callison RYA Architecture, Seattle, WA

PHOTOGRAPHY
Courtesy of RYA

Parkson, with more than 70 locations in Malaysia, China and Vietnam, is one of the most prestigious department stores in Asia. For its newest store, in Kuala Lumpur, the Lion Group (owners of Parkson) called upon the designers at RYA (now the Callison RYA Design Consultancy), to create what they hoped would be "a shopping experience that would be unparalleled in the region." On this site in the Golden Triangle of Kuala Lumpur, the designers were "to develop a canvas that would allow the merchants to showcase Parkson's point of view through the strong use of lifestyle presentation and visual display." To achieve their design ends, RYA took a holistic approach, and created the retail brand strategy, planning design, merchandising program, and the graphic communications for the project.

The large gridded windows that serve as a perimeter wall of the cosmetics department allow the daylight to stream in and increase the brightness in the white-on-white space. Simple cube-like counters and fixtures play off geometrically against the square white columns that create merchandising bays within the department. Some of the counters are highlighted with veneers of a soft, warm beige color.

While white and soft neutrals predominate throughout the multi-level store, the shopper is more aware of the numerous mannequins that "people" the store; on ledges, standing alongside fixtures filled with components of the featured outfits, or clustered in life-like groupings on, or near, stylish pieces of furniture that suggest the lifestyle.

Changing colors and flooring materials helps to delineate one area from the other. Most areas are illuminated by the recessed ceiling lamps and some adjustable spots are used for highlighting display features. The massive square columns that punctuate the floor become decorative focal elements as they are treated with patterns, artwork, and materials that help to "explain" what is in the area or who the area is for.

The rounded edges of the plastic floor fixtures in the young people's shop are white and lime colored and, along with a blue denim color, help to define this department. The colorful murals painted on the columns continue the denim color and are accented with beige and warm browns. Besides the headless mannequins standing on the floor there are dozens of male and female white abstract mannequins on view on the ledges, showing off the latest in mix and match outfits.

A small, deep red area rug on a square of black flooring provides the focal setting for the intimate apparel shop where realistic mannequins are grouped about, and resting on, a curvaceous couch. Black wall accents and fixtures complement the white floors and ceiling and make this shop distinct and unique.

The designers said: "Our aim was to create a high concept destination emphasizing connection to the local culture, merchandise presentation, customer service amenities, and meaningful entertainment destination." By the crowds that fill the aisles of this store one must concede that the design team at RYA ably succeeded in fulfilling their objectives.

Palacio Acapulco

Acapulco, Mexico

DESIGN
Pavlik Design Team, Ft. Lauderdale, FL

PHOTOGRAPHY
Courtesy of Pavlik Design Team

The Palacio de Hierro department stores, as designed by the Pavlik Design Team of Ft. Lauderdale, are always outstanding retail designs no matter where in Mexico they are located. For the beach side mall in Acapulco, in the noted Mexican beach resort, the Pavlik designers had to covert a former parking garage with low ceilings into the semblance of an upscale specialty lifestyle store. Since Acapulco is primarily a vacation and "weekend" city, the merchandise focus is on fashion accessories, gadgets, gourmet and lifestyle essentials for "the casual upscale shopper."

In order to make the store more welcoming, the limestone and glass façade was extended into the adjacent blank wall space with shallow display windows set in— "making the mall front appear much larger." Inside the store, a wide curving boulevard with overhead ceiling coffers creates an easy, open flow that visually opens up the low, U-shaped space. The 8 ft. high ceiling neatly contains the perimeter light troughs, the accent lighting and the recessed coffers that reinforce the flow of the curved central aisle. The floors are kept light and neutral in color—cream, taupe and white porcelain tiles—in order to

create an overall unified feel. The modular frames on the perimeter walls are backlit frosted glass with white, high-gloss niches "creating sleek neutral backdrops for the colorful merchandise vignettes." It is the merchandise itself, in varied and colorful display arrangements that entice the shoppers and lead them through the store. Warm wood feature frames and columns punctuate the clean interior and create special merchandise focal points. These modular perimeter frames combined with the versatile fixturing "create total flexibility for the ever-changing merchandise stories that vary throughout the year."

Despite the small, low space "every inch was maximized with built-in storage modules and rotating panels that contain merchandise and graphic components to vary the presentations." All these elements, taken together and as expertly combined by the design team, "create a unique shopping experience for the vacationing, casual upscale shopper."

Shopko
Green Bay, WI

DESIGN
Chute Gerdeman Retail, Columbus, OH

PRESIDENT
George Nauman

CREATIVE DIRECTOR/ENVIRONMENTS
Brian Shafley

EXECUTIVE VP, ACCOUNT MANAGEMENT
Wendy Johnson

VP BRAND COMMUNICATION
Adam Limbach

DIRECTOR VISUAL STRATEGY
Bess Anderson

DIRECTOR DESIGN DEVELOPMENT
Steve Pottschmidt

TRENDS & MATERIALS SPECIALIST
Katie Clements

DESIGNERS/BRAND COMMUNICATION
Matt Jeffries, Elaine Evans

DESIGNER/GRAPHIC PRODUCTION
George Waite

PHOTOGRAPHY
Image Studios, Appleton, WI

The designers of Chute Gerdeman Retail were challenged by Shopko, a multi-department value retailer, to design a new generation store—"a fashion forward concept" that would appeal to their core shoppers: women who are driven by value, convenience and family. The 80,000 sq. ft. store in Green Bay is the result of that design process and has already won first prize in *Chain Store Age's* "discount store/mass merchant" category. It is warm and welcoming and strikes a balance between practical components and aspirational elements.

The prototype design is a complete re-think of the whole store experience. It includes everything from the brand identity and exterior store architecture to the interior design, fixtures and graphic communications. The new logo design acknowledges the "female focused brand position" and the original heavy, red and blue logo has been replaced by a more sophisticated, "more feminine and fashion-forward aesthetic with an earthy palette." The interior has softer elements as well with "rounded visual cues that

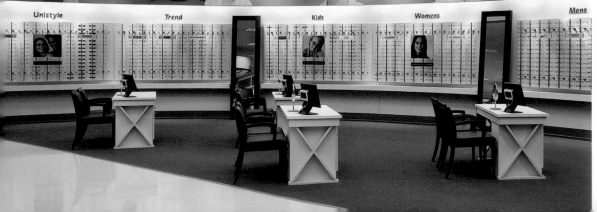

are integrated with the high service touch points and way-finding strategy." Now, moving through the store is a more relaxed and stylish experience and the interior features a new "landscaped" approach "to optimize story-telling opportunities." Fashion related products are positioned at lower levels—in the center of the store—while stackable hard goods are displayed on taller gondolas. Thus, since "outfitting her family is important to her," the items for the entire family are readily seen as the shopper enters into the new store.

"Dramatic boutique focal points" appear at the entry to each of the store's major departments. They "help break up the big box feel and make the store easier to shop." Each focal point helps guide the shopper through the store "encouraging her to shop multiple departments

by showcasing Shopko's quality merchandise." Color also plays a crucial role in helping to distinguish departments. The Chute Gerdeman designers added "residential" touches to enhance the new design and make it more enticing for female shoppers. There are now armoire-type fixtures, lamp shaded lights, coffered ceilings, and special woodwork details like picture rails and crown moldings. Also, lifestyle imagery is layered into the merchandise presentation. "The framed lifestyle imagery is displayed on the integrated rail system around the perimeter of the store—in a way the shopper might display pictures at home. To quote the designers—"It's her life, her style, her store!"

Topshop/Topman

Lower Broadway, New York, NY

DESIGN
Dalziel and Pow Design Consultants, London, UK

CREATIVE DIRECTOR
David Dalziel

TEAM LEADER FOR INTERIORS
Felicity Pogson

TEAM LEADER FOR GRAPHICS
Scott Albon

PHOTOGRAPHY
Andrew Townsend

Such excitement! Such anticipation! Such expectations! And — finally it arrived! "It" is the new Topshop /Topman store that arrived in all its sparkle, shimmer and English Pop swagger and swish. "IT" is the new Mecca for the 20-to-30 crowd — the in place — the hot spot — the right spot. The store, designed by London based design firm Dalziel and Pow, brings pizzazz and color and the very latest in British fashion to fill the almost 35,000 sq. ft. space on four floors in a vintage cast iron building on Lower Broadway where it joins other "in" shops. The street is evolving into the Land of Oz for the young shopping crowd.

For the just-out of high school (or college) traveler who made it to London — backpack and all — it's like coming home again. The visual excitement of the Topshop store on Oxford Street in London has been transformed and transferred to the classic facaded store in New York, "a perfect space for contemporary retail." According to the design team at Dalziel and Pow, in addition to the high ceilings "each floor features the original metal columns, set off against the clean, crisp ceiling and wall treatments. Topshop flooring is a combination of tile and timber; the tile giving some pace through the middle of the space and the timber a nod towards the original specifications."

The entrance has been extended over the three upper floors. The new glazed atrium, above the lobby, serves to emphasize the scale of the space.

A full height glass wall separates the escalators that are set to the right side of each floor and they are "merchandised to maximize the impact of the fashion on offer." The graphics on the escalator wall also serve as a tie-in with the "mother store" in London and this new, big, sprawling New York babe. There is a photographic montage that features London icons and references to Topshop and Topman culture. "The escalator is framed by a new directory system we trialed in White City, and becomes particularly effective here given the complexity and size of the store." Navigational signage within the store follows the same fun, crisp and informative/illustrative style.

Color is tops in Topshop. Whether it is the merchandise or the colorful graphics that seem to compete for wall space, everywhere the eye comes to rest there is something of interest: a mannequin dressed in the latest look, a giant photo blow-up, a dangle, or one of the original classic iron columns. Whatever the eye misses is made up by other sensual elements such as the sound of music or the whiff of a scent in the air.

On each floor there is a play of light and dark as elements on the floor and ceiling are juxtaposed. A white ceiling raft that runs the length of each level is complemented by the white tile "avenue" below it. The ceiling feature stands out from the balance of the ceiling that is painted a dark gray, just as the white "avenue" contrasts with the deep gray stained wood floors. "The overall ambience is dramatic and theatrical accentuated with directional spotlighting throughout and the relatively low light levels."

Each floor has its own custom designed wall system and fixtures and they not only add interest but help to define areas. "Specific product zones or sub-brands get their own treatments, creating the impression of a fluid and varied space that will be constantly evolving — constantly on trend."

While Topshop is devoted to women, Topman gets its own domain in the basement. As described by the designers, "It is a more intimate space crammed with visual interest and character. The ceilings are lower here and this adds to the feeling of immersion — a club-like vibe — which is part of the brand's heritage. Departments and product stories are arranged around the perimeter, and a glass box in the middle of the floor creates a space that is intriguing but instinctive to shop."

To some — perhaps many — Topshop/Topman is a totally new and strange phenomenon. Outside of the Oxford Street store in London, this is the brand's "strongest statement." Back at the end of the 18th century, the British crossed the ocean but lost the Colonies. This time, with this retail phenomenon and the exciting retail presence — the Brits may win back some of what they lost.

Fairweather

Square One Shopping Centre, Toronto, ON, Canada

DESIGN
Ruscio Studio, Montreal, QC, Canada

PRINCIPAL
Robert Ruscio

Though it meant reducing the square footage of Fairweather's space in the up-scaling Square 1 Shopping Centre, it also meant upgrading the Fairweather operation and reaffirming its brand as "a sense of fresh and contemporary fashions, affordability and assortment." Ruscio Studio of Montreal was called upon to redesign the store.

The new look of Fairweather, a popular priced chain of stores for women's fashions, is now housed in this 8,000 sq. ft. space and boasts a new façade that extends up from 11 to 18 ft. and with its dark matte/subtle glossy stripes, the façade achieves "a bold look that can now be clearly noticed from a distance." The windows are brightly illuminated to showcase the featured garments.

The 17 ft. runway or catwalk — at the entrance — brings the window displays into the store. "Instead of being greeted by a barrage of packed floor fixtures, customers immediately notice the latest collections available." Focal points help to distinguish the various areas within the shop. The floor is now the "whitest porcelain available" and that high glossy reflection "evokes a sense of women's fashions." Custom cut vinyl appliqués on the white walls not only add a contemporary look, but also provide a sense of style. The brushed black chrome finish of the large round columns "anchor the eye to the mannequins in front of them."

Basically, the sales area is white with black accents while the fitting rooms are the opposite with dark panels of wallpaper, soft pendant lighting, black leather poufs and rich, warm exotic wood floors. The result is that this area becomes "more personal and intimate for the customers."

"Visual breaks" interrupt the white perimeter walls which now house seven categories; Isaac Mizrahi, MIKK Couture, Fiorucci, Majora, Beekers Brook, coats and dresses, and accessories. Black, backlit arches in the foreground frame the merchandise collections and "create a feature presentation space for each particular section." The designers added backlit fluorescent lighting behind the wall elements, including the mirrors, arches and floating walls. Wall washers and track lighting with ceramic arc metal halides highlight feature areas and displays.

"Through the renovation of the store, the merchandise now appears more fashionable. By keeping the merchandising approach, by presenting it in a way that is more current, Fairweather was able to maintain the affordability aspect of their brand." The Fairweather name has been revitalized as the buzz that surrounds the new look of the store makes apparent.

Adessa

Oberhausen, Germany

DESIGN
Plajer & Franz Studio, Berlin, Germany

PROJECT MANAGER
Brigit Tuermer

PHOTOGRAPHY
Fotostudio Arnolds gmbh, Aachen, Germany

When the management of Adessa, a chain of fashion stores in Germany and Europe, called upon the designers at Plajer & Franz Studio in Berlin to design a new "trendsetting retail concept" for their stores, the goal was to "strengthen the brand recognition and presence in the market while staging an exciting lifestyle shopping experience" for their shoppers. The newly designed store environment certainly promotes the company's slogan: "Fashion for Family."

Seen through the open façade are large, lifestyle images that announce that this is a family store. "A fresh new lightness of colors and materials, clear zoning and circulation on the floor and ceiling, and effective arrangement of the individual segment brackets engage the customer and beckon her to step inside." There is a "fashion boulevard" that functions as the main axis for the store's layout, and the central area brings together the individual sub-labels and it

"represents the family meeting point." Surrounding the central round table, highlighted by its "lifestyle" lampshade, are the especially designed tall cabinet-like fixtures for accessories that also serve as "totems" on the floor. The fixtures are whitewashed wood accented with the brand's signature red and blue colors, and the units contrast with the dark, zebrawood floors. Adjacent to this central accessories area is a raised platform for modern women's and young fashions. Women are the main target group for Adessa's fashions for the family and this area is further accentuated by the floor-to-ceiling blue striped wood claddings.

The new logo, graphics and communication systems were also developed by Plajer & Franz. "The new color scheme and design vocabulary fuses all five elements of the parent brand into the Adessa family, consistently reflecting the same principles as the store concept."

POP
Munich, Germany

DESIGN
EXPOLAB, Munich, Germany

PHOTOGRAPHY
Marek Vogel

Expolab of Munich is an agency for multi-dimensional brand communication, interior design and exhibit design. It took all the combined efforts of the design firm to come up with the retail design concept for POP—Munich's newest "hip individualist fashion boutique." This shop was designed to complement POOL (a shop we reviewed in our October 2006 issue) and the design team decided that "clean surfaces, graphic contrasts, deliberate use of color, and quirky details demonstrate the idiosyncratic character of POP." With its wide range of trendy street wear, POP has a slightly younger feel than its "elder" sibling—the POOL shops. To interpret this new brand, the designers teamed Pop Art, comics and surface design in a very contemporary manner.

Black elements meet arctic white surfaces to affect a clubby ambiance where bright yellow accents "underline the graphic impressions and present a strong backdrop for stylish labels. "The shop is organized on two levels—one towards Sendlinger Strasse and the other to Dultstrasse — and on either level the shopper is greeted by "a firework of visual surprises and special features." Through the use of

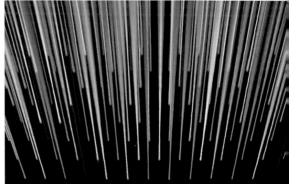

mirrors, the custom-made light installation appears to "extend indefinitely." This "Rush of Lights" consists of a multi-colored optic fiber cable that spans two kilometers and runs through various levels. When the Rush of Lights is combined with music, it comes to pulsating life, and with the different programming modules creates exciting light shows to delight and intrigue shoppers.

According to the design team, "Cut-out forms create airiness among the furnishings, reflections and shiny surfaces work a kind of graphic magic. The shop's mascot is a giant gorilla — sawed in halves — and the King of POP is turned into a cash desk. He also welcomes the ambitious shopper at the Dultstrasse entrance. Shopping is POP — so let's POP!"

M Penner
Uptown Park, Houston, TX

DESIGN
Michael Malone Studio @ WKMC Architects, Dallas, TX

PRINCIPAL IN CHARGE
Michael Malone AIA

PROJECT MANAGER
Steven Domingue, Assoc. AIA

PROJECT TEAM
Alesha Niedziela Assoc. AIA

Paul Pascarelli Assoc AIA

Karen Evans, Assoc. AIA

CLIENT'S REPRESENTATIVE
Senterra

PROJECT TEAM
Neil Tofsky, Rob Sigler, Matthew Goldsby

PHOTOGRAPHY
Jud Haggard Photography

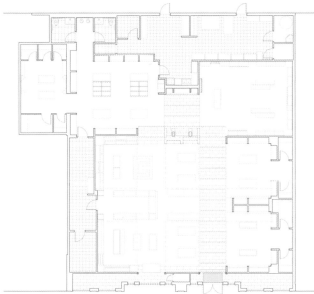

M Penner has presented the most fashionable and the finest of European clothing to men in Houston, TX. for the past three and a half decades. According to Michael Malone, of Michael Malone Studio @ WKMC Architects of Dallas, the store has had "a contemporary point of view and a strong fashion direction supported by impeccable taste"—and these were the qualities he had to make self evident in the new 8000 sq. ft. store he designed for the company in Uptown Park, Houston.

The original store was designed primarily as a clothing store with multiple levels and was poorly adapted to the display of sportswear—a category that had become one of the company's fastest growing areas. There was no room for expansion in the shoe and accessories area and the newly introduced women's wear was stalled for lack of space and acceptable dressing rooms. Thus, the new store—double the size of the previous one—instead of compartmentalizing merchandise categories "allowed each department to flow seamlessly into a larger merchandise mix. Organized as one contiguous open space, defined by floor fixtures and ceiling fixtures, the space is expansive but carefully divided into subtle groupings around category and lifestyle." From the entry, circulation flows in a modified racetrack and the Zegna shop draws shoppers to the rear of the space. A stone and marble main aisle serves to lead shoppers to the various areas in the store. Since sportswear, as a category, is so important at M Penner, it is located up near the entry and fills in the cen-

ter of the racetrack. The fixtures here include open legged, marble topped tables and rolling bins on casters that make relocation fast and easy.

The women's shop appears—prominently—on the left of the entry. The wall hanging units are visually treated similar to those in the men's area but there are floor cases for accessories and T-stands for dresses and gowns. There are also two spacious, salon-sized dressing rooms for the women.

Also given prominence up front is shoes. There are illuminated shelves for the display of men's shoes along with a wall for socks and belts making a major statement for footwear and leather goods. A bench, used for fitting the shoes, was especially designed for this store and the back of the unit is a flat tabletop for display. More accessories and specialties, such as cuff links, fragrances, eyewear etc., appear as part of the cash/wrap counter that is located adjacent to shoes. The long counter can be used to service several customers at the same time and illuminated towers, on the back of each side, show additional small items.

The shirt and tie area consists of two walls of shirts on illuminated shelves and a massive, tiered tie display table. There are also tables where shoppers can assemble the shirts and ties that go with the suits or jackets the shopper has selected. This section is located immediately off the clothing area and "this completes the pattern of circulation."

The previously mentioned Zegna shop, at the rear

of the store, was especially designed for the M Penner shop. It is separated from the clothing area by the made-to-measure space with its conference table for the lay-down and display of fabric books and catalogues. Built-in shelves, along one of the walls, holds reference materials and samples of the custom lines available in this shop. "Like many better men's stores, made-to-measure has a role of growing importance to M Penner and provision of a dedicated area for this activity was central to the design."

In the clothing area, illuminated wall bins with adjustable standards for the hang rods hold the suits and sports jackets. The center of the floor contains the pants racks and the lay-down tables for mix and match. The dressing rooms are clustered around a large fitting room with seating provided for those who wait. A wet bar provides the hospitality in this area— "which is still the backbone of the business."

White-washed oak was used for all the fixtures and the wall paneling, except in the Zegna shop. The oak is accented with brushed aluminum hardware and trim. Thin panels of backlit alabaster form a valance over the hanging clothes bins and indirect fluorescents are used in the bins and the light coves. Metal halides serve for the highlighting and displays. "The result is a cheerful, open, comfortable yet sophisticated place to shop that fits the beautifully made things on sale in the store and the welcoming warmth and expansive nature of the owners—Murry and Karen Penner."

Best
Dublin, Ireland

DESIGN & FITTINGS
Umdasch Shop Concepts, UK

PHOTOGRAPHY
Courtesy of Umdasch

Best is a chain of 15 men's fashion-forward shops located in Ireland and the stores are synonymous with exclusive brands of men's fashions such as Hugo Boss, Tommy Hilfiger and Lacoste. According to the designers at Umdasch Shop Concepts UK office, who were responsible for the design, layout, fixtures and fittings, "The Irish retailer sees itself as a personal advisor and is thus particularly interested in long term customer relationships." Though the Best shops are usually in top shopping centers, this two level flagship store is located on Mary St. in Dublin — an up and coming shopping street. "The target customers here are youngish with a cosmopolitan flair."

Though the floor plan is a long and narrow space, the designers found a "witty" solution in the serpentine elements that ooze their way through the floors and "catch the customers' attention as they wend their way through the sales area and skillfully (the lines) divide the range of goods into sections." As the shopper gets deeper into the shop — past the staircase up front that leads to the upper level — "the more strongly these ribbon-like elements become interlinked." The aim was "to arouse the interest of the shopper and encourage him to continue into the interior of the store and thus explore the areas at the back as well." The casualwear is here on the entry level while the more formal clothing — suits and such —are on the upper level.

The "white ribbon" band effectively divides the

wood paneled walls of the shop into clusters or groups and in the "dips" where the "ribbon" drops down before going up to create the next bay, the space becomes a focal area where a dressed hanger can display a completely accessorized outfit.

The company's red and blue signature colors appear amid the natural wood tones on the floor, the wood squares applied to the long perimeter walls, and to complement the flowing white ribbon. The red color appears on the rear wall, on both levels, where it leads to the dressing rooms. The rich blue color lines the stairwell between the two levels and blue

fabric is used to upholster the man-size chairs set out on the floor. Blue feature displayers share the center floor with the clubby seating, and white abstract mannequins use the displayers as resting points.

Though the ceiling is polka-dotted with incandescent lamps, almost all of them can be focused and used to highlight the wall displays as well as the feature floor fixtures and the dressed mannequins.

Paul Stuart

Oak St., Chicago, IL

DESIGN
Charles Sparks & Co., Westchester IL

PRESIDENT & CEO
Charles Sparks

EVP ACCOUNT EXECUTIVE
Don Stone

DIRECTOR RESOURCE STUDIO
Rachel Mikolajczyk

DOCUMENTATION COORDINATOR
Olivia Lindenmayer

RETAIL DESIGN TEAM
COO
Jack Freedman

GENERAL MANAGER
Blake Johnson

PHOTOGRAPHY
Charlie Mayer, Oak Park, IL

Most major cities have their high fashion streets and in Chicago the street to be on if you are a class retailer is Oak St. Oak St. runs perpendicular to Michigan Ave.—the Magnificent Mile—and sits at the gateway to Chicago's truly elegant Gold Coast. This street is filled with charmingly scaled buildings, many from another era. Some have been updated, "modernized" and others still show their age. It is into one of these turn-of-the-century townhouses that the noted men's shop—Paul Stuart—has been relocated.

Many years ago Retail Design International featured the Paul Stuart store that filled the first two stories of a Michigan Ave. skyscraper. With occupancy costs rising and opportunities for greater operating efficiencies, the retailer commissioned the Charles Sparks design firm of Westchester, IL. to find a new location and "reinvent" the Paul Stuart operation. "Once the 6500 sq. ft. Oak St. location became reality, our (the design team's) challenge was to design, document and build the new Paul Stuart."

The new location meant going from 23,000 sq. ft. to 6500 sq. ft.—on two levels, and as for the building—it required a total renovation of interior décor finishes, new millwork and fixtures, a restoration of the floors and the building's façade. "Because of the narrow scale of the

space, in lieu of built-in niche cabinetry against the walls, we opted for a more open panel approach that allowed more exposure for merchandise while also widening the space." The millwork design is "a classic modern aesthetic" and the English oak is finished with a medium tone stain. It features "a shifting fluting to create a motif inspired by the proprietary Paul Stuart weave pattern" that is part of the company's branding. In contrast to the woodwork, a light mustard color was applied to the walls and ceilings. Rust-colored area rugs and runners, by Missoni, with edges bound in leather cover parts of the restored travertine floors. A handsome, traditional wood banistered staircase connects the two levels of the shop.

According to the designers, "The 'townhouse' aesthetic takes the iconic Paul Stuart brand and updates it for a new generation." The shop maintains "a classic elegance that remains in the reinventing, along with the timelessness of true luxury, the bold new face that will serve a modern, increasingly discriminating customer." With this new design in the new more compact but efficiently and effectively used space, there is more focus on personalized service which seems to be what the Paul Stuart client wants.

Wrangler

Madrid, Spain

DESIGN
Dalziel and Pow Design Consultants, London, UK

ASSOCIATE DIRECTION INTERIORS
Marcus King

INTERIOR DESIGNER
Juan Diaz Del Castillo

PHOTOGRAPHY
Courtesy of Dalziel and Pow/Wrangler

This Wrangler store, designed by Dalziel and Pow Design Consultants of London, was the first of a rollout for brand stores as well as vendor shops in other retail establishments. It opened on Fuencarral — a major shopping street lined with top fashion and brand name denim stores.

"This concept aims to reignite the brand, creating a unique retail experience for Wrangler's customers and a template for further European development. The new scheme makes use of raw honest materials such as cast concrete, concrete screed, rough sawn oak, and distressed yellow metal to selected fixtures—to develop a contemporary and chic atmosphere." The sliding, frameless glass door system folds away to provide a view into the store as well as free access. An industrial roller shutter, over the entrance, carries the Wrangler brand signage when the shop is open and a large scale brand image by a local graffiti artist when the shop is closed. A special lighting system was developed to fit into the random plank ceiling of the store and it also serves to link the three areas of the shop. Large scale wall graphics are applied in key areas on the concrete walls.

On the first level up there is a showroom and meeting area that serves Wrangler's to-the-trade operation. Combined with the retail store at ground level, this location offers a brand experience to trade buyers and consumers alike.

Underground
Market Mall, Calgary, AB, Canada

DESIGN
Ruscio Studio, Montreal, QC, Canada
DESIGNERS
Robert Ruscio, Marie-Eve Belveau
PHOTOGRAPHER
John Bilodeau Photography, Calgary, AB

Though Underground originally catered mainly to men, the new look created by Ruscio Studio of Montreal, was created to attract and increase sales in the women's area. As the name suggests, the inspiration for the shop in Market Mall in Calgary, AB was the subway—an urban icon.

Setting the underground, tunnel-like feeling are the curved glossy white tiled walls on the left side of the shop as seen through the wide entrance. It is these white walls and the introduction of female mannequins along with the colorful graphic posters that make the women's area more attractive to women: certainly more than the previous black and dark stained wood treatment. The store's feature design element is "the continuous and metamorphic 64 ft. long 'metal ribbon.'" It starts up front as a tiered platform for mannequins and merchandise and then "draws the customer in

as it transforms into other functions allowing one to interactively walk over or under the metal sculpture." This focal element is "raw" with one side clear metal, and collaged with posters on the other. Throughout the space "street hoarding posters" and large full-size "branded posters" appear and speak out to the shoppers. "Real street hoarding posters give off a city core urban feeling."

Raw materials appear all through the space—rugged urban textures that in their "rawness" still are smooth, sleek and sophisticated. The concrete floors are smooth and polished and though the space is dark and dimly lit, it is dramatic and theatrical rather than "dark." The white tile wall that runs along the left side of the shop where women's wear is contained, is gently curved as it

reaches up to the blacked-out ceiling. The stainless steel covered arcs that separate the wall into story or category segments add a graceful note while reinforcing the subway imagery. Also adding to the subway theme is the exposed yellow fluorescent strip lighting that can be seen from the mall and that continuous along the perimeter walls in the men's area.

The success of the new Underground store design has been phenomenal — according to the sales reports.

Edwin Watts Golf

Concord, NC

DESIGN
JGA, Southfield. MI

VP, CLIENT STRATEGIES
David Nelson

CREATIVE DIRECTOR
Kathi McWilliams

CLIENT'S TEAM
VP
Bill Grigsby

VP, MARKETING
Lincoln Cox

DIRECTOR RETAIL DEVELOPMENT
Jerry Gibson

CONSTRUCTION MANAGER
Therese Huggett

APPAREL BUYER
Helly Scharf

DIRECTOR OF VISUAL MERCHANDISING
Dennis Sarp

ARCHITECT
Space Planners/Architects, Monroe, LA

PHOTOGRAPHY
Laszlo Regos Photography, Berkley, MI

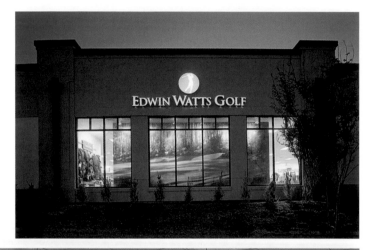

The objectives for the design of the new Edwin Watts Golf store in Concord, NC were quite direct; "translate the client's love and understanding of the game into a branded prototype of visual focal points that convey their authority in the sport" while showing the merchandise brands in an ambiance easy and pleasurable to shop. Also — facilitate simple and consistent roll-outs of this design for future retail spaces.

The freestanding 9700 sq. ft. building has numerous windows that allow shoppers to see into the store while drivers get their first glimpse of the store from the signature murals on the rear of the building. The use of warm wood tones suggests a sophisticated country club environment and the interior design by the JGA of Southfield, MI design team brings the outside in — "making the buying experience as much fun as a round of golf."

The interior is divided into three focal areas: shoes and apparel, equipment. and personal service. The self-serve shoe department serves as a bridge between the men's and women's apparel areas and points up the distinctly separate shop for women. In the equipment zone, flexible divider bay walls along with an adjustable graphic rail system allow Edwin Watts Golf to accommodate the ever changing spatial requirements for the merchandise brands they feature. Adjacent to this area is the personal service zone that is anchored by the Edwin Watts Golf Academy. Here, in an open and welcoming space, shoppers can test products with Visual Golf Simulators or get personal instructions or have equipment especially fitted to the customer.

A putting green, between the two focal areas, creates an

interactive element in the design. Putters can be tested here. At the rear of the shop is a comfortable seating area and entertainment is provided by golf-related broadcasts and a dramatic wall of framed photographs. A scent machine provides the aroma of freshly mowed grass to complete the outdoorsy atmosphere.

To create the desired indoor-outdoor ambiance, there is a fieldstone wall near the entrance and it backs the cash/wrap while imparting a signature element to the brand. The color palette selected by the JGA team includes a sunny yellow, accent green walls, chocolate/cherry wood toned flooring and green, grass-like carpet-ing — all to "bring the outside feel inside." Near the golf club fixtures, the designers specified recycled rubber flooring to resist the wear and tear of the clubs striking the floor.

The new design provides a simplified custom fixture system that readily adapts to varying merchandise and satisfies the need for vendor branding. Nesting tables are used to create focal points throughout. These focal points are enhanced by track lighting "enabling merchandise to be featured in a more impressive style."

Addict

Covent Garden, London, UK

DESIGN
Brinkworth, London, UK

For their first retail store outside of South-ampton — to be located in the trendy Covent Garden area of London — Addict asked the Brinkworth design team, also of London, to "reflect the sophisticated graphic picture of the brand" in their design. Thus, Brinkworth's design team has created a monochromatic background to highlight the product present-ation. The designers used "an urban, muted color palette of black, gray and white through-out the two floors of shop, contrasting the flat, smooth painted walls against the original, worn wooden floors upstairs (street level) and the utilitarian gray-painted concrete floors down-stairs." The emphasis is purely on product and the unique, specially commissioned artwork.

The entrance is mostly black and it is illum-inated by a light raft that continues through the shop interior to the rear of the space. Sus-pended backlit screens and white light boxes run parallel to the black raft. Matte black powder-coated oval tube steel was used to create a specially-designed fixturing system that includes free-standing units, wall mounted rails and a double height shelving system. The latter runs down the side of the staircase—from ground level to basement—and thus provides a sense of continuity between the two levels. "All modules intelligently interconnect to allow full adaptability for the varied products in the Addict range."

The Addict logo is laser cut into one side of

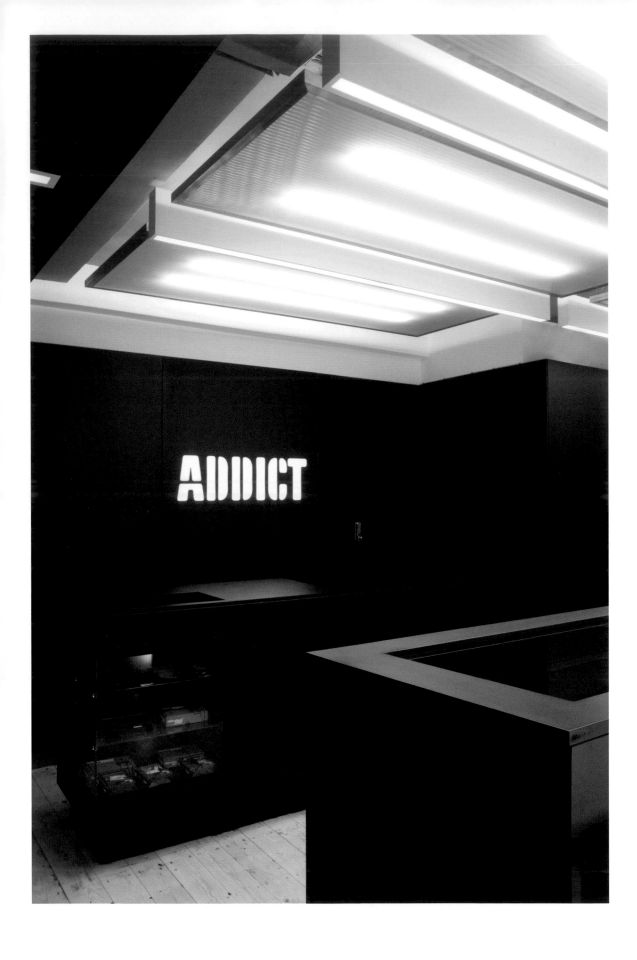

the uprights of each display fixture and the "understated branding" continues with a simple, backlit logo above the black box that serves as the cash desk.

The Brinkworth designers created a series of focal areas in the store for product promotion that can be redressed easily and frequently. One is the large floor-to-ceiling display cabinet on the ground level. It is made of glass and mirror "arranged to bounce graphics around the store." Another is the custom designed light box on the wall of the staircase that allows Addict to temporarily exhibit the collaborative artwork that is integral to the brand.

Kevin Brennan of Brinkworth said, "We carefully considered the graphic nature of the Addict brand and every aspect of the interior reflects this—from the subtle branding of the display units to the installations by the artists."

Mom & Me

Ahmedabad, India

DESIGN
Dalziel and Pow Design Consultants,
London, UK

DIRECTOR, INTERIORS
Keith Ware

INTERIORS PROJECT LEADER
Andy Piepenstock

ASSOCIATE DIRECTOR, GRAPHICS
Chloe Beach

SR. DESIGNER, GRAPHICS
Lyndall Coburn

PHOTOGRAPHY
Andrew Townsend

The Mahindra Group have established themselves as a recognizable name in the children/soft toy market in India, and with the increasing growth of retail opportunities in that market, Mahindra and Mahindra decided the time was right to establish their first retail brand. The niche they opted for, and which they felt was ready for development, was the mothers and children's area. "The group identified a gap in the market for stores that provide a high standard of products, ambiance, value-added services and customer service to mothers, babies and older children." The result, as shown here, is Mom & Me with clothing and hard goods for children up to nine years of age and expectant mothers.

Dalziel and Pow, the London-based design consultants, created the brand identity and the retail environment for the new brand. A name was generated — Mom & Me — with the "&" used as the brand icon and as part of the communication system throughout the store and on swing tickets.

For the store interior, Dalziel and Pow created "a memorable and fun corporate identity with a warm palette of materials "to appeal to the female customer." White is predominant on the walls and ceilings and is accented with warm, wood tones and assorted peach/beige and off-white giant squares on the floor. The over scaled photographs and color-filled graphics add a lively and fresh feeling to the space.

The store opens with a glazed shopfront and a wood-veneered ceiling raft that floats overhead from the entrance to the cash/wrap at the rear of the store. "A unique and flexible hanging merchandise system is fixed to the ceiling raft, which maximizes product display and visual merchandising opportunities." The varying floor and ceiling treatments, the color accents and the graphics all help to clearly define the many different "shops" in the store.

Adding to the communication system are the large environmental graphics — photo images of children — that form backgrounds for focal bays or walls. Some of these images appear to be wrapped around columns turning them into identifying "totems" on the sales floor. To reduce the potential clutter on the floor and to ease customer flow — mothers with push carriages, carts, strollers or children in hand are a major concern — a simple merchandising system is used on the walls and mid-floor.

The lighting levels are carefully controlled to add contrast and more warmth to the scheme. White semi-abstract mannequins, fully outfitted, appear on low platforms set out in the main traffic aisles. The same simple risers are used to feature hard goods items as well.

In addition to maternity clothes and apparel for infants to nine year olds, there are areas in the store devoted to nursery and children's furniture, transports, travel, safety, and games and toys.

A flagship store for this rapidly growing chain is in the works in Delhi. "No other brand in India offers such a diverse and affordable product range and Mom & Me is set to become the market's leading one-stop for mother and children's products."

GreatDreams

Shenzhen, China

DESIGN
rkd retail/iQ, Bangkok, Thailand
Rkurt Durrant

CLIENTS TEAM
CEO
Jonathan Wang

CORPORATE BUSINESS UNIT DIRECTOR
Tom Hammer

MARKETING DIRECTOR
Clara Gao

BUSINESS DEVELOPMENT DIRECTOR
Eric Lu

RETAIL DIRECTOR
Candie Yang

REGIONAL STORE OPERATIONS MANAGER
Tiger Xing

FRANCHISING SENIOR MANAGER
Steven Ni

PHOTOGRAPHY
rkd retail/iQ

Greatdreams is a children's lifestyle specialty store located in Shenzhen, China. The space, designed by RKurt Durrant and his rkd retail/iQ team of Bangkok, is almost 56,000 sq. ft. and carries a wide variety of apparel, accessories, furniture and toys — all the things that make up a child's world. The purpose of this design, that targets the wants and needs of two-to-12-year-olds, was to take this significant catalogue of merchandise that goes across all categories and develop a multi-retail format that would showcase the merchandise. Howie and Landau are very recognizable and much loved cartoon characters in China and very popular with children of all ages. It is these two characters and their adventures that served for the decorative aspects of Greatdreams' design.

The cartoon characters are out in front of the bright red façade ready to greet the young shoppers. They reappears over and over again as the families make their way through the many shops-within-the-shop that make up this vast complex. Cut-out silhouettes of Howie and Landau serve as special entranceways for children and up front — near the entrance — is a carousel-like feature with an orange drum upon which assorted cartoon characters appear. Radiating out from this are bright yellow metal fixtures filled with assorted games, toys, plush animals and stationery. The shoe area is highlighted by a floor-to-ceiling open wall shoe display and an orange colored recessed ceiling above the interlocking multicolored chairs brings focus to this area. There is a TV monitor to distract children while shoes are being tried on. Throughout, the space is light and bright: lots of

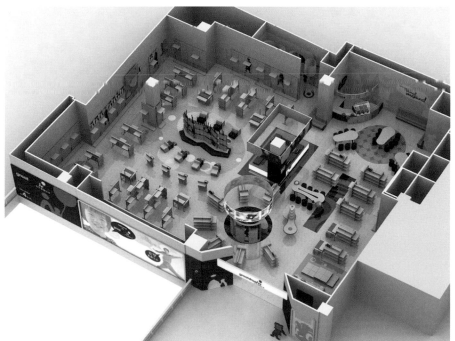

white on walls, floors and fixtures accented with strong primary and secondary colors that also help to define the different shop areas.

According to RKurt Durrant, the designer, "Family love and bonding through shared experiences were core values identified early in the process and applied to all aspects of the shop concept." Since expansion of the retail brand is currently in a "go" mode in China. Greatdreams will be appearing as free standing shops or as a shop-within-a-shop boutique form in selected department stores. All the design elements were directed towards this brand expansion. As Durrant states, "Retail formats were developed across a variety of real estate opportunities and brand positioning exercises." Thus, the design was developed "to showcase the children's apparel, and home and lifestyle merchandise in an easy to shop experience-oriented, lifestyle specialty store called Greatdreams."

Magic Attic

Derby, UK

DESIGN
Dalziel and Pow Design Consultants, London, UK

PHOTOGRAPHY
Courtesy Dalziel and Pow Design Consultants

Magic Attic, so named by Dalziel and Pow, the London based
design consultants, is an off-shoot of the Save The Children
organization. The concept was to raise the profile of Save The
Children, showcase their work, and connect more closely with
local mothers and children "in a welcoming and special retail
environment." This store design was originally intended to be
located next to the organization's charity shops and was "to
delight children and engage adults."

Though the initial design called for a space of 1000 to
1800 sq. ft., the design — as shown here in Derby — is only
750 sq. ft. The store was refitted to include new and recycled
products for children and pregnant women. In addition to
books, toys, clothing and equipment, there is a selection of
healthy drinks for sale as well as Fair Trade coffee and home
made snacks. An important area in the shop is the activity
zone where children can play, be kept amused and occupied
while also "raising awareness of some of the vital work going
on worldwide by Save The Children."

As is to be expected, Dalziel and Pow was also severely
challenged by a very low budget. To quote the designers: "We
decided to create a dramatic focal point in the scheme with a
strong architectural form anchoring the cash desk and promotional stock, finished in bright orange Marmoleum." The

rest of the scheme relied heavily on bright, strong colors and amusing graphics. Working within set guidelines, custom graphics were designed to suit the brief "to delight children." There is a game set out on the floor — somewhat like "snakes and ladders" — but designed to play up Save The Children issues, a fun height chart, and a magnetic map of the world. The latter can be used to show artwork done by children in the store.

Featured in the store's window is the Yak gondola: a life size, cut-out yak that not only is a merchandise displayer, but holds topical graphics. It greets shoppers out on the street with a welcoming smile. The yak is also a reminder that for a donation of 160 pounds (about $255.) a hairy yak can be provided to a family who will gather its wool, its milk and also get a hearty assist from the animal when it comes to ploughing the fields.

Dalziel and Pow undertook this assignment on a "not for profit" basis; operating at cost and the suppliers who were involved in producing this shop either contributed things at cost or at heavily discounted prices. With the assist of suppliers such as I Guzzini (lighting), Stylo Graphics (environmental graphics) and MZK (merchandising systems, mid floor gondolas and the yak), the store was fitted on budget — recycling as much of the existing material as possible — and in just three weeks. As Dalziel and Pow says — considering it was a new concept and included a new accessible toilet and baby changing area — "Not bad!"

Faith

Westfield Darby Mall, UK

DESIGN
Dalziel and Pow Design Consultants, London, UK

STORE CONCEPT & DESIGN
Guy Smith, Duncan Lane

BRAND POS. & ART DIRECTION
Chloe Beach, Lyndall Coburn

The designers at Dalziel and Pow Design Consultants, the London based design firm, explain their approach to the design of the new shoe store as follows: "Faith are targeting a more sophisticated and aspirational customer and they briefed us to evolve their brand accordingly. Our initial work helped redefine the brand's positioning and once we established a clear understanding of the required tone and attitude, we began to design the elements that would deliver the new approach."

Shown here is the result of the new design for Faith as it appears in the Westfield Darby Mall in Darby. Dalziel and Pow started with a new logo for main signage and branding, and the interior design combines techniques used both in designer boutiques as well as volume retailers. For the shopfront, the display windows have been reduced in width to form two narrow glass columns that flank the wide, gracious entrance to the shop. A cluster of display plinths — columns of assorted heights — are positioned at the entry and serve both as a feature "window display" and as merchandisers. These elements "allow customers to effectively 'shop the window'."

Two massive glass screens, up front, display key elements of the store's collections and while one points up the "Top 10" selling products, the other promotes Faith's new premium Solo range. In the center of the shop interior, a black and bronze "glass room" has been created as a dramatic centerpiece. This contains the "boutique" or Solo selection of products in the store. Around the perimeter of the space, soft white panels curve from floor to ceiling "radiating light and presenting the stock against a neutral background."

The new packaging — also developed by Dalziel and Pow — builds on the white/bronze color scheme of the shop and completes the palette with warm grays and yellow for the core collections and black and purple for the Solo designs.

Distinguishing the store is the photography done under the art direction of Dalziel and Pow. It sets the tone for brand communication both in-store and in the fashion press. "Mixing the grit and glamour of paparazzi photography, the new images exude a glamorous, sexy lifestyle caught as if unaware through a telephoto lens." The new store is simple and easily understood but its design not only distinguishes it from the competition — it also redefines the Faith brand.

Rockport
Ramat-Aviv Mall, Tel Aviv, Israel

DESIGN
Madesign, Tel Aviv, Israel

ARCHITECT/DESIGNER
Michael Azulay

PHOTOGRAPHER
Yaki Asaiag

Michael Azulay, the principal and architect/designer of Madesign in Tel Aviv, was faced with a dilemma. His question: "How can the will of the designer to convey his talent and abilities, while creating new shapes and making surprising use of materials, coexist with the product being sold without taking the attention away from it?"

With the Rockport store in the Ramat Aviv Mall in Tel Aviv, Azulay appears to have found his answer. There is a hint of the 1970s in the simple, rounded shapes of the drywall construction yet with the warm, wood-flavored wallpaper Azulay creates "a familiar, pleasant place." As he said, "The structure accompanies the wall of the space and drapes

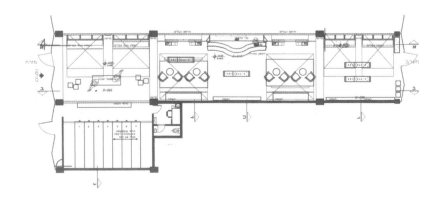

them from within, softening the dwelling feeling and creating an atmosphere that is nothing like the feeling of visiting a simple, square space."

Defining the two separate spaces that make up the shop are two overlapping rounded layers: one in shades of brown and one in white. "In addition the complexity of the inner layer and the unique atmosphere, much thought has been given to the placement of the shoes. The main focus here is the shoes, and they stand out in their presence. Combining the brown shades with the neutral whites alongside the soft lighting, allows the full collection to be displayed, without creating visual deficiencies and esthetic hazards."

The design comes across in the large constructions of the space and the 34 shoes are displayed in a simple and approachable manner "which allows them to receive the shoppers' full attention."

Cross

Natick Collection Mall, Natick, MA

DESIGN
RGLA, Schiller Park. IL

PRINCIPAL
Joseph A. Geoghegan, Jr.

PRINCIPALS
Randy Sattler, Robert Arend

DIRECTOR OF CLIENT SERVICES
Nancy Newport

SR. PROJECT ARCHITECT
David Heidtke

SR. DESIGNER
Ed Hanlon

MANAGER OF MARKETING & CREATIVE SERVICES
Ivelisse Ruiz

DESIGN ASSOCIATES
Bill Dodge, Michelle Krause

ARCHITECTURE ASSOCIATE
Stephanie Weber

CLIENT'S TEAM
VP STRATEGIC DEVELOPMENT
Robin Boss Dorman

VP GLOBAL MARKET
Chad Mellon

DIRECTOR GLOBAL MARKETING
Tom Peterson

CREATIVE MANAGER
Kristine Lauer

VISUAL MERCHANDISING & STORE PLANNING
Peter Paulo

CREATIVE SERVICES MANAGER
Duane Doorakian

RETAIL OPERATIONS
Sandy Sidoti

BUYER
Wendy Leviele

PHOTOGRAPHY
Robert Nash

Looking to appeal to "a younger, female demographic," the well known A.T. Cross Company — an established manufacturer of fine writing instruments and accessories — asked the designers at RGLA of Schiller Park, IL to design a new retail concept. Cross has a history of over a century and a half of "reinventing writing instruments and combining design ingenuity with jewelry like craftsmanship." That store design was inaugurated in the Natick Collection Mall in Natick, MA. Designed to communicate the new image of Cross while also referencing the distinguished heritage of the brand, the new design in the 900 sq. ft. space delivers a contempo-

rary setting with a residential feel. It also gives the brand "a platform for self-expression and a venue for its lifestyle-infused product collections."

The design team of RGLA, working closely with the Cross team, created a series of signature elements that can be adapted to future Cross retail stores. The gently curved storefront with its cool accent lighting "expresses a more feminine aesthetic" and the adaptable and easily changed module cube system in the window "complements the style and grace" of the Cross products. The cubes also bring the small items up closer to the viewer's eye level. "Everyday luxury" is introduced on the shop's interi-

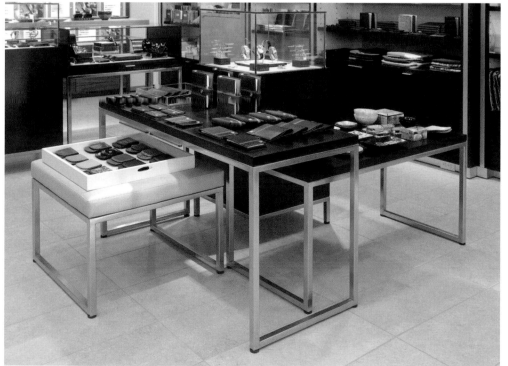

or where fine fabrics, quilted leather and quartz composite countertops are used.

These are complemented by the selection of fine light and dark wood accents and the decorative pendant light fixtures. Display trays are set out atop ottomans "to further advance the welcoming, comfortable feel of the store." Located at the rear of the shop is a dramatic—yet informative—"pen wall." The built-in display of illuminated graphics and the customized fixtures help to educate the customer in their choice of pens. The pens can be tested at conveniently placed flat surfaces.

The Cross line now includes, in addition to the writing supplies, other accessories and gift ideas such as timepieces, cuff links, eyewear, leather accessories, stationery items, desk sets and computer tote bags. These are presented on contemporary floor fixtures and in alcoves with open glass shelving for easy-to-touch accessibility.

The prototype store has proven so effective and successful that other Cross stores following this design concept are currently opening across the country.

Skarbiec Jewelers

Krakow, Poland

DESIGN
Ovotz Design Lab, Krakow, Poland

CURRENT DESIGN DIRECTOR
Wojciech Stanczykiewcz

PHOTOGRAPHY
Jakub Kaczmarczyk

Located in a rather ancient building in Krakow, Poland that stands amid many other historic and centuries old buildings is the new shop of Skarbiec Jewelers as designed by the local design firm, Ovotz. The client's objectives were simple and direct: create as large an exposition area as possible in this 110 square metre (about 1150 sq. ft.) space that will contain "exceptional functionality and a modern feel that will complement the existing historical interiors."

Despite its Gothic origins, the building has been subtly altered over the centuries and currently has a 19th century look. Since "the façade is an integral part of the project and follows the aesthetic of the interior, a subtle balance of old and new was born," said Wojciech Stanczykiewicz, currently the Design Director at Ovotz. The façade is now painted gray and off white and accented with plum and bronze trim. The large, floor-to-ceiling, frameless glazing of the display window — "shaped as a sort of box emerging from the facade" — gives an excellent view into the shop.

"The most challenging part of the work was to generate a modern interior capable

of co-existence with the historical structure already present." The designers chose materials such as basalt, granite, bronze, aluminum and a variety of exotic woods to "set the basic aesthetic temperature later completed with custom-designed showcases, window arrangements and lighting solutions."

The original 18th century plastered walls and ceilings were "renovated" and finished in an "uneven off-white color" and the accent walls that housed the showcases were finished in a deep taupe/gray. Gray flamed basalt and granite tiles cover the floors and the fixtures were constructed of bleached oak and teak, and accented with bronze and aluminum. Some of these fixtures appear against the dark walls while others are hung as displayers or are free standing near the shop's entrance. There are two cash/wraps and they also serve as showcases for some of

the store's products.

Light plays an important part in this design. According to the designers, "The light design is based on direct delivery of light and by doing it so the original details of the ceiling can be respectfully underlined. Direct light application can only be found as a dedication to two free standing showcases appearing at the entrance and also above the two cashier's desks. Since there is a significant impact of external light, changing according to the seasons, block dimmers have been applied for a smoother regulation of light intensity."

The new design artfully and respectfully bridges the centuries and creates a sophisticated minimalist/modern interior in a centuries old shell.

Key West

Ste. Catherine St., Montreal, QC, Canada

DESIGN
GHA design studios, Montreal, QC

PRINCIPAL
Steve Sutton

SENIOR DESIGNER
Marie-Francoise Fourcand

SENIOR TECHNICIAN
Jerry Cabaluna

ARCHITECT
Stoa Architects, Montreal, QC

PHOTOGRAPHER
Yves Lefebre, Montreal, QC

Key West's merchandise mix focuses on high fashion brand sunglasses and sports watches. This store, located on heavily trafficked Ste. Catherine St. in Montreal, is the flagship store for the chain and was designed by GHA design Studios, also of Montreal. It was designed "to solidify its role as the sunglass and sports watch authority" and highlight the company's emphasis on top name brands.

GHA created the new logo for Key West and it is featured throughout. On the façade, the logo "wallpaper" is applied as a film to the inside of the glass. On the interior of the store the "wallpaper" extends up from the top of the display units and surrounds the shop's periphery. The long narrow space was dealt with by having the product display along the long walls and only two narrow, illuminated display cases share the open

central area with the shoppers. The cash/wrap — located at the very rear — also avoids a bottle-neck situation in the middle of the store. "Every effort was made to visually open up the space as much as possible by raising ceiling heights to the structural deck and creating a black and white 'light-box' of a store with dashes of racing stripe red on the floor to draw customers towards the rear of the store."

All the merchandise units have backlit LUMI-SHEET panels illuminated by integrated LEDs. "The dark colored products appear to float on the white illuminated surfaces." Each pair of glasses has a magnetic tag attached to it that sets off an electric alarm if the product approaches the front door. That cuts down on shrinkage especially since the store is located in a busy, downtown location.

Using a black and white palette, all the materials are contemporary. "A layering effect along the store perimeter is achieved via a creative application of transparency and luminescence." The feeling is of a "luminous space" and it is underscored by the backlit white panels previously mentioned, and the white lacquered fixtures and wall units. These are complemented by the white floor highlighted with the red dashes. The new Key West logo is adapted as a wallpaper pattern and applied over the cases with transparent glass panels offset a few inches from it by stainless steel spacers. Against the black painted ceiling deck and black top tier wall, the white drywall ceiling seems to float and the black ventilation duct runs down the center of the space to become an effective element in the design.

DESIGN
Chute Gerdeman Retail, Columbus, OH

PRINCIPAL
George Nauman

DIR. OF VISUAL STRATEGY
Bess Anderson

SR. DESIGNER OF ENVIRONMENTS
Steve Calhoun

SR. DESIGNER OF BRAND COMMUNICATIONS
Steve Boreman

DESIGN, BRAND COMMUNICATIONS
Mary Lynn Penner

FOR ROSS-SIMONS
CEO
Darrell Ross

DIR. OF STORE DESIGN & CONSTRUCTION
Tracy Zaslow

Ross Simons
Providence Place Mall, Providence, RI

The design team of Chute Gerdeman Retail of Columbus, OH was challenged by Ross Simons to "create an environment that anticipates the needs of each customer and provides an intimate, relaxing space that encourages socialization and provides surprises to shoppers along the journey." The end of that "journey" would be "the thrill and excitement of a jewelry purchase." Ross Simons has been providing exceptional quality jewelry at most affordable prices for almost six decades.

The team focused on making the 2500 sq. ft. space in the Providence Place Mall in Providence, RI "approachable" — warm and inviting. The peek-a-boo windows set in the hand applied, faux stone finish of the façade gives shoppers a view into the store. "The grand, over-scaled double doors mimic the Ross Simons jewelry box when closed, and when opened — resemble the inside of the box, complete with the jeweled chandelier nestled

inside like a sparkling treasure." The luxurious Ross Simons packaging, as noted above, was used as the inspiration for this new retail store concept. Rich chocolate brown, mint green and platinum serve as the color palette. "Chocolate was used as inspiration because buying a piece of fine chocolate is not unlike buying jewelry — both are small, delicious treats where presentation is key." The rich brown colored carpet sets off the pearlescent wall coverings and also highlights the Rolex area. Brown — along with the soft green — appears in the suede fabrics used inside the jewelry cases.

The cases are positioned at various heights to give shoppers "a feeling of discovery." The cases have platinum painted legs, and modern pearlescent finished abstract mannequins and forms are used to point up Ross Simons' fashion-forward and trendy merchandise from around the world.

The bridal area features a sit-down, curved

counter and the gentle arc of the fixture is repeated on the ceiling overhead. "Upholstered chairs and new lifestyle graphics encourage customers to relax and enjoy the life-changing purpose (engagement and/or wedding rings)." Up front in the store is the Rolex area accentuated with the chocolate brown mosaic tiled wall framed with velvet drapery. This space was designed to be "unique, masculine and upscale." The area "evokes a sense of destination" and the bar height counter and upholstered stools make the watch buying process more personal and comfortable.

Chute Gerdeman has provided Ross Simons with a "journey" worth taking.

Stark & Whyte

Montreal, QC, Canada

DESIGN
Ruscio Studio, Montreal, QC

SENIOR DESIGNER
Robert Ruscio

INTERIOR DESIGNERS/PROJECT MANAGERS
Marie-Eve Beliveau, Andrea Temple

GRAPHIC DESIGNERS
Jessica Fiorella, Noe Sardet

ARCHITECT
Richard Prud'homme Architecte, Montreal, QC

PHOTOGRAPHER
Yvan Dube, Longueuil, QC

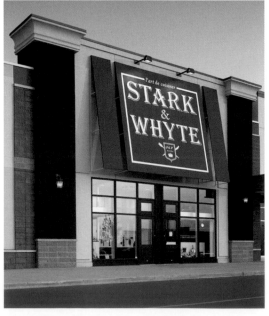

Ruscio Studio, the Montreal based design firm under the creative direction of Robert Ruscio, was called upon to create, not only the new retail store design, but the entire branding for the new Stark & Whyte kitchen/cookware venture.

According to Robert Ruscio: "The first thing we wanted to do was render authenticity. 'Stark' is Philip Stark, the client but 'Whyte' is a fictitious name that lends an traditional, old-British trading center quality to the name." The font was chosen to create that bygone 19th century look, and the logo is an armor crest with thin borders in vanilla over chocolate brown. The shop had to go beyond being a place that sold goods. It had to be a "unique shopping experience" and always have something new for the shopper to experience. According to Ruscio, "The biggest feature and brightest idea was to create an operable kitchen island at the front of the store." With cooking classes, daily tastings and wonderful aromas, it makes a great opening statement into the contemporary and sleek store. In keeping with the teaching, tasting and learning concept, there is a 16 ft. long communal table complete with cook books, pencils and note pads where "clients can be inspired and get creative with new cooking concepts."

The deep, rich chocolate brown of the logo is also the dominate color on the shop façade as well as the store's interior. The wood floors are stained a deep, dark brown and same signature brown covers the walls. The canvas valances that stretch across the ceiling and effectively block out the dark painted ceiling and camouflage the HVAC systems create a more human-scaled feel to the shop. These horizontal bands are made of the same awning fabric that dominates the façade. The valances also contrast with the vanilla-colored shelves, cubbyholes and assorted fixtures and display tables that sparkle in contrast to the brown surround. The Stark & Whyte logo appears in several locations inside the store including the giant exhaust enclosure over the central kitchen/work space. An occasional white framed grid unit is suspended from above over one of the display tables and it carries lighting to highlight the displays below.

The design must be partially credited for the success of the store and the capacity classes conducted here by local hotels staffs and culinary schools. In addition, there is a sense of adventure and the possibility of discovery in this store which is a mix of "a big box discount store and a brand name boutique."

Sabon Spa
Eilat, Israel

DESIGN
Madesign, Tel-Aviv, Israel
Michael Azulay

PHOTOGRAPHY
Courtesy of the architect

According to Michael Azulay, the principal designer/architect at Madesign of Tel-Aviv, "The concept was to maintain the recognizable look and feel of the soap store, but to give it a make-over in order to create an atmosphere of an elite and unique boutique for pampering care products. In the past, the stores were targeted at gift shoppers, but today the store sells products for personal day care." With that in mind, Azulay and his design staff approached the new design for this Salon Spa in Eilat — a tourist attracting location. Salon Spa is a chain of shops — 21 in Israel and 20 abroad—that offers a wide selection of products pertaining to bath and personal care.

The designers wanted to maintain "the existing colorful and familiar look and feel" of the chain while making the new shop as unique as possible — providing "an innovative feel and amplifying the purchasing experience." The shopfront design is different for this location from those surrounding it in the mall but is similar to the façade design used in the stores abroad. "The storefront welcomes the customers before they walk in." It is constructed of "rustic wood" and with display platforms that create "a glass-fronted display cabinet." The pine wood has been stained to affect an aged look.

In an attempt to connect with all of the shopper's

senses, the designers placed a well with streaming water in the center of the space to appeal to the sense of touch. The sense of smell is stimulated by the assorted pleasant aromas emanating from the products presented on the walls. For the sense of taste — "there is an illusion that the products are edible since they have aromas that are familiar to us, and they are displayed in an appetizing way—like in a luxury delicatessen." The products are appealingly set out on the shelves of the dark wood armoires or cabinets that line the walls. These cabinets have a "vintage look—as if they were collected from various sources and connected together." The cabinetwork in each is unique with details such as crown moldings, cornices, ornamental legs and laser cut decorations and/or signage. The cabinets are constructed of oak and the shelves are backed up by panels of luxury wallpapers. The wallpapers vary according to the product display on the shelves. The color palette for the store is made up of warm neutrals; white, vanilla, chocolate brown, gray, almond and the natural oak.

The focal element in the shop — the well — is a stone sink constructed of aged cracked stone layered over a wood frame. It is highlighted with custom designed brass faucets and pedals. The soft residential lighting adds to the rich, warm ambience of the shop.

DFS Galleria
The Shoppes at The Four Seasons, Cotai Strip, Macau

DESIGN
rkd retail/iQ, Bangkok, Thailand

CLIENT'S TEAM
PRESIDENT GROUP EAST
Tim DeLessio

MANAGING DIRECTOR HK DIVISION
David Charles

VP, WORLDWIDE STORE DEVELOPMENT
David Gester

VP, BUSINESS DEVELOPMENT
Kevin Tranbarger

VP, GLOBAL VISUAL MERCHANDISING
Graeme Fowler

STORE DEVELOPMENT MANAGER
Andrew Gibb

STORE PLANNING MANAGER
Dicky Chan

PHOTOGRAPHY
Hans Schlupp

There was a time, not too long ago, when anyone looking for total immersion gambling would have headed to the island of Macau, off the coast of mainland China. But Macau's vision of itself is evolving, and, with the addition of the Cotai Strip, the complete, beyond gambling, Las Vegas experience is becoming a reality in this part of the world.

With direct connections to the Four

Seasons Hotel Macau and the Venetian Casino, the new DFS Galleria, designed by rkd retail/iQ of Bangkok, promises to be the most complete luxury shopping destination in Macau. The complex focuses on retail brand assortment and presentation, and, with 60,000 sq. ft., anchors the entire ground level of the retail podium.

Building on the directive of ultimate luxu-

ry, rkd retail/iQ developed a concept of progressive experiences. "Boutique" galleria comprises 18 of the worlds' top luxury brands, while "Beauty" showcases 24 of the best cosmetics, treatment and fragrance brands. In the "World of Luxury" there are three areas of luxury boutiques consisting of six of the very finest jewelry brands, an impressive line-up of watchmakers and leading brands in fashion accessories.

RKurt Durrant, president of rkd retail/iQ notes, "A further departure from the traditional DFS was the inclusion of significant neutral and non-selling architectural spaces. The introduction of 'palette cleansing' transition zones showcase artwork, offer the opportunity for periodic change and provide a positioning element for DFS to express their artistic personality to complement the luxury retail environment."

Award panels from around the world have taken note of DFS Galleria: it won first place in competitions run by both the Retail Design Institute and Chain Store Age. It also won Grand Prize from the Association for Retail Environments, Specialty Store over 25,000 sq. ft.

Lefel

Via Cavour, Parma, Italy

DESIGN
Crea International, Milan, Italy

CLIENT LEADER
Alberto Pasquini

DESIGN DIRECTOR
Camilla Croce

STRATEGY DIRECTOR
Viviana Rigolli

STRATEGIST
Marco De Carli

LEAD DESIGNER
Sara Rimini

ARCHITECT
Marcela Mangupli

LEAD GRAPHIC
Sonia Micheli

GRAPHICS
Serena di Fidio

PHOTOGRAPHY
Courtesy of Crea International

If you live in Italy, the name LaFeltrinelli may be familiar as a specialist in books, music, games, travel and luggage. When LaFeltrinelli decided to expand and create a new brand, they contacted the creative talents at Crea International of Milan to bring the new concept to life. For the name of the new brand, UE! Communications came up with "Lefel." "The name, a soft verbal symmetry anchored to a strong center, arises from the world of LaFeltrinelli and opens it towards new dimensions. The brand combines the rigor of font with the game of capital and small letters so to interpret the personality of the new sign speaking to a cultured and refined consumer."

The pilot for the new retail concept is a 3,380 sq. ft. store on the Via Cavour in Parma. It has its own signage, furniture, and layout and also its own specific merchandise. Camilla Croce, Crea International's Design Director explains the approach she and her team took to the project: "Strongly believing that style is secondary to sentiments in order to make our surroundings more human and ethic, I thought of how I could create an effective relationship between customers and the spaces they interact with. It's that precise link which pushes us to come back to shopping to the same place."

Based on that "wooden box," a new modular format was developed that will adapt to almost any space. Made of oak, walnut and wenge wood are the assorted sized rectangular, open-faced boxes that can be stacked in myriad ways and in unlimited combinations to suit the product offer and the wall bays allotted. According to the design team: "Wood with its warmth wrap the environment, using the space effectively." The same assortment of boxes can and are used as tables, dump bins, build-ups, and risers out in mid floor. While the perimeter walls are made of stacks of these assorted rectangular "blocks" filled with stock, the stack-ups in mid-floor feature new arrivals and special promotions. A "lab tree," made of modular overlapping elements is used to attract shoppers and the LCD screens implement the communication process.

As for fixturing Croce explains: "Everybody, me included, has an old wooden box at home full of keepsakes and experiences we can dip into for hours. Lefel is a dream container where anyone can listen to enchanting stories told by a free and adventurous spirit. A spirit who collects and shares them with kind hearted people who believe in effective connections with everyday life objects."

Throughout the two floors of the store the natural woods of the boxes is complemented by a white surround and the sharp red signature color that pops up in the signage, directions and decorative accents.

Graphics play a major role in the Lefel environment. They were conceived to offer the shopper a "journey" inside the store since the travel concept is of prime importance to the product mix. "The leading idea of travel is then transferred graphically in the postmark as a sign of something that can be brought home after a journey that transmits strong emotions." Alberto Pasquini, Chairman of Crea International puts it this way, "We have succeeded in giving birth, spirit and shape to Lefel — interpreting it as a strong, brave and ageless women, capable of traveling independently — who faces life and makes strong decisions with determination and enthusiasm." Lefel invites you along on a travel experience that never takes off but never leaves you behind.

Telefonica

Madrid, Spain

DESIGN
Brandimage Desgrippes & Laga, New York, NY

CREATIVE DIRECTOR
Maki Schmidt

PHOTOGRAPHY
Courtesy of Brandimage

Located in a 1920s building that was probably the first skyscraper built in Madrid, is Telefonica's new retail and exhibit space designed by Brandimage, Desgrippes & Laga of New York City. In addition to representing the company's brand equity, it also serves as an experiential learning center that shows how "technology is relevant to people today and how they can best integrate it into their lives."

The flagship store occupies two floors in the building. The retail space on the ground level presents mobile and fixed line phones, TV services, prototypes and telecommunication packages, audio visual services, live content broadcasts, as well as areas for internet experimentation and a special game/play area for children. Up on the first floor, in the House of the Future, visitors are invited to see the technology that is important for consumers and small business owners. This floor also houses a service center where consumers may interact with Telefonica's support staff and an auditorium that can accommodate one hundred guests. The company plans to eventually open the next two floors to exhibit Telefonica's art collection, present temporary exhibits of interest and host cultural events.

Renee Peet, Executive Director of Brand Strategy at Brandimage said: "Telefonica presented us with a unique challenge in that their desire was literally to 'invite' people into their brand and help them understand how to best use technology in their lives. We wanted to create a forward looking environment to accomplish this, in keeping with the technologically-advanced nature of the brand, yet ensure that it was friendly and accessible, and maintained the intrinsic qualities of the historic building they were housed in."

The two floors currently in use are connected by "an innovative promenade staircase designed as an inviting area encouraging visitors to congregate." Multimedia screens connect the experiences of the ground and first floor and "serves as a metaphor for the Telefonica brand equity of connecting people with technology and helping them experience in a new way."

Brandimage approached this project holistically, beginning with strategy and going through graphic design, fixtures, language and architectural design. "Virtually all services the company uses were brought to bear. The result is not only a tangible representation of the Telefonica brand equity, but the creation of the major technology exhibition space in Spain — if not in all Europe," adds Ms. Peet.

Hamley's
Dubai, UAE

DESIGN
Chute Gerdeman, Columbus, OH

PRINCIPAL
Denny Gerdeman

CREATIVE DIRECTOR, ENVIRONMENTS
Brian Shafley

EXEC. VP ACCOUNT MANAGEMENT
Wendy Johnson

VP, BRAND COMMUNICATIONS
Adam Limbach

DIRECTOR, VISUAL STRATEGY
Bess Anderson

DIRECTOR, DESIGN DEVELOPMENT
Steve Pottschmidt

TRENDS & MATERIALS SPECIALIST
Katie Clements

SR. DESIGNER, BRAND COMMUNICATIONS
Steve Boreman

DESIGNER, BRAND COMMUNICATIONS
Matt Jeffries

DESIGNER, GRAPHIC PRODUCTION
George Waite

RETAILER'S TEAM, HAMLEY'S LONDON
TRADING DIRECTOR
Paul Currie

GROUP HEAD OF VM & DESIGN
Colin Morrisey

Hamley's has been a beacon for children of all ages for over two centuries and the tall, proud Hamley's building on Regent Street in London is a must-see landmark. The designers at Chute Gerdeman of Columbus, OH were invited by the noted toy retailer to create an "experiential and innovative kit-of-parts concept" for the company so that it could expand globally. The new design concept had to expand on and develop from the London heritage — but with a twist, It had to be distinguishable through signature elements, create a strong brand identity, make use of "strong, bold iconic statements to create a lasting impression and make the store design and product mix relevant to the diversity of today's kids the world over."

The new concept was introduced in the Dubai store. To convey the brand to this new audience, the design team blended elements of the Hamley's of London brand with the world of story-telling for children. The seven floors of the London store were "compressed" into the single floor in the Dubai mall and "a meandering discovery path" leads shoppers through the space with wall murals and full height focal points serving as directionals and stopping points. Making a strong color statement is the glossy red — Hamley's signature color — along with metallic gold, rich wood cabinetry, clear acrylic globes and an assortment of natural trees and faux foliage.

As for the fixtures, they are part of the store's ambiance. "The environonment package is flavored with hints of Dubai culture. Hamley's branded steamer trunks and demonstration tables mix it up with exotic, dress-up cabanas, radio-controller car rally features, a floor-to-ceiling doll house, and a flower-shaped tot's play park. The high capacity, gold-plated fixtures that incorporate comprehensive graphic systems are often located in hands-on focal areas.

All the cash/wrap stations support an "Old London" look, but, as evidenced throughout the color-filled and adventure-saturated space, all are done with a fun and fresh attitude. The London-with-a-twist concept is boldly expressed in the graphics which presents the numerous famous brand names of the toys, games and dolls and yet lets the Hamley's brand rules supreme. "Stylized, London-inspired wayfinding elements are playful yet regal, and work their way into the customer journey." Visual and graphic elements are supported with hands-on interactive focal elements or activities: In a larger-than-life way they make the journey through the store a special treat.

What the Chute Gerdeman team produced is "a distinctly regal Hamley's London fixture and visual package that even when merchandised with unique Middle Eastern appropriate toys, still enhances the overall fun, global, kid-like atmosphere."

Colorlab Custom Cosmetics

Chicago, IL

DESIGN
Wells Design Group, Bartlett, IL

PRINCIPAL
Kent Wells

PHOTOGRAPHY
Charlie Mayer Photography, Oak Park, IL

In 1996 Mary Swaab, a noted make-up artist, brought her cosmetic lab to the counter with a system that could create custom lip shades in any texture. From there she launched Colorlab Custom Cosmetics and now she has opened her first U.S. boutique on Armitage St. in Chicago. As designed by Wells Design Group of Bartlett, IL, the luxurious space features a clean white backdrop for the cosmetics with white floors, walls and ceiling accented with candy pink, purple and blue "that reflect the brightness of the product and the packaging."

Kent Wells, the principal of the design firm, said, "Soft neutrals and unique textures were used to create a contrasting backdrop to the vivid colors that dominate Colorlab's identity." The individual make-up stations set out on the floor are defined by cranberry colored circles and circular ceiling "clouds" floating overhead. These "clouds" support customized LED lighting and cascading prism chandeliers.

The primary interaction between the "inventor" (the consultant make-up artist) and the client occurs at these "pods." "They are designed to allow for semi private consultation." In addition to the lighting previously noted, the pods are equipped with large mirrors, comfortable adjustable stools, and a display of pigments and make-up products easily accessible to the "inventor."

"The space for the flagship store is multi functional as the environment needed to be flexible and adaptable to allow for retail sales, inventor training and private events," said Wells. The success of this shop has helped "this innovative and experiential brand" to grow rapidly—"transforming cosmetic counters nationwide into dynamic, engaging and interactive centers of make-up creation."

Bullseye Bodega
The Art of the Pop-Up Shop, New York, NY

DESIGN
David Stark Design, New York, NY

PHOTOGRAPHER
Patricia Willis

Pop Up shops have been popping up with more and more frequency over the past several years. It was only three years ago that we reported on the Pop Up shop created for Comme Des Garcons, the celebrated Japanese design firm, in a run down — but up and coming Berlin neighborhood. Pop Ups have become a way of retail life around the world and especially for Target in the USA.

Basically, a Pop Up shop is a temporary shop. It is not designed to last. It is not permanent. It is planned to disappear and not be heard from again — until something new, different and newsworthy is about to happen. Success does not mean it stays open! The Pop Up will often appear in an otherwise unrented space on Main St.—or in a mall—often without too much fanfare except for maybe newspaper ads—and posters spread across the shop windows. Trendwatch, an internet service, states, "If new products can come and go, why can't the stores that display them do the same? Well, you guessed it — retail outfits increasingly do. From gallery-like shopping spaces with one-off exhibition to mobile units bringing inner-city chic to rural areas, Trendwatching.com has noticed an increase in temporary retail manifestations around the world." These are the Pop Up shops!

Target has been dubbed, in the US, "the king of Pop Up retail." Only a year or so ago they opened a 1500 sq. ft. shop in Rockefeller Center for one month only to promote the special line of clothes designed exclusively for Target by Isaac Mizrahi. The same company took advantage of an open space in the Bulls Eye Inn in the Hamptons — an upscale resort area just outside of New York City—to set up a temporary casualwear shop for five

weeks only during the summer months to catch the weekenders and others who could use the clothes that Target had to offer. In June of 2008 there were "Deliver the Shiver" Target bulls-eye logo-ed trucks out in Times Square — for one day only—selling brand new 5000 BTU air conditioners at $75 each — and each came with its own Bulls Eye pull away cart — free.

The newest Target Pop Up concept, shown here, is the Bulls Eye Bodega. As the Target press release announces it is "the launch of four limited time only stores that celebrate the retailer's pioneering designer partnerships and commitment to offering amazing value through unique and differen-tiated merchandise programs." Taking a playful spin on the traditional and familiar sight in many New York neighborhoods — the bodega — the local corner grocery/convenience store that usually caters to the Hispanic local markets. These four stores, designed by David Stark Designs of New York City, amusingly recreate the Bodega's crowded, product-overloaded ambiance with cartoon graphics, kitsch signage and commercial metal/wire fixtures. The designer products are shown amid the clever "packages, cans and cartons" and they average at about $25! These stores are offering the limited-time collections that include Anya Hindmarch handbags, Sigerson Morrison footwear and Jonathan Saunders GO International fashion collection.

The four Bodegas had graphic announcements posted out front — some on the bus stops in front — and their windows were covered bodega-style with brightly colored signs. The stores were cluttered with simulated bodega merchandise along with the real products. Real fun! Real New York City! And Really a Pop Up shop!

Point Zero

De la Gauchetiere West, Montreal, QC, Canada

DESIGN
GHA design studios, Montreal, QC

PRINCIPAL
Steve Sutton

SENIOR DESIGNER
Serge Labrie

SENIOR DESIGNER
Aki Kechagias

DESIGNER
Zahra Peal

FIXTURES, MANNEQUINS & FORMS
Adco, Montreal

ARCHITECT
Groupe Archifin, St. Lambert, QC

GENERAL CONTRACTOR
Multi-Renovations Gendron & Assoc., Longueuil, QC

PHOTOGRAPHER
Yves Lefebvre of Yves Lefebvre Photography, Montreal, QC

This was a rather special pop-up shop, not for a week, or a month, but to be open for four months. After that four-month stand in this location it was to be replaced by an actual retail store for the same client. According to Steve Sutton, the principal at GHA design studios of Montreal, "The idea behind building the pop-up shop was to generate hype and excitement for the brand and the upcoming opening of their flagship. Point Zero wanted to have stores that support the brand's merchandise and reflect its philosophy of 'Luxury for Everyone.'"

Since the Point Zero brand is already known, accepted and popular, and found in major department stores and independent shops across Canada, the company did not want its pop-up shop to look "temporary" or look as though the company was in "transition." Thus, for this limited installation, the designers at GHA specified custom fixtures, wall merchandising systems and lighting fixtures — all to be dismantled in four months. Driving the design was the strategic and large scale use of illuminated graphics — some of which reached 15 ft. in height and whose impact was felt from the street. "The graphics act as a beacon to lure customers into the brightly lit space."

There were restrictions on what could and could not be done with the store's shopfront, so the objective for the design team was to embark on "an ambitious build-out" during this pop-up stage — "giving it maximum visibility and having the finished façade ready when the store opened officially." To define the strong brand statement that this store caters to young, fresh, and energetic men and women, the previously mentioned oversized illuminated graphics appeared close to the store's windows. The interior of this landmarked space features very high ceilings and the designers capitalized on that height for platform build-ups filled with white, semi-realistic mannequins parading in the newest fashions. The square columns that divided up the open space were either wrapped in the colorful graphics or painted white like the walls, ceiling and floor. Most of the fixtures, furniture and the sky-high drapery that separates the dressing rooms were also white. Almost everything about the shop was white except for the bursts of color that jumped off of the graphics and the outfits on the mannequins that seemed to be everywhere in the store. The graphics were "powerful visual statements and were an effective tool in creating 'a big

bang for your buck.'" They also supported and reinforced the message that appeared on bill-boards out on the highway, on the bus shelters as well as on the busses themselves — along with the ads in the fashion magazines — all part of the Point Zero marketing campaign.

The pop-up store opened without any advertisements and the buzz was generated by word of mouth and the sales were in line with projections. This was "in itself a testament to the store's success, given that Point Zero has no previous stores and there was not a publicity campaign dedicated to the store opening."

So — you are thinking — whatever happened to all the stuff that was created for the pop-up store? As the designers said, "all the merchandise displays were designed with the knowl-edge that they would be eventually replaced by the fixtures that will be in the flagship." Those used in the pop-up were transported and used to furnish other pop-up shops — in To-ronto, Vancouver and Calgary — where they too heralded the arrival of a new Point Zero flag-ship store. Nothing was wasted — just reused and repurposed along the way.

Piazza S. Jacopino

Arezzo, Italy

DESIGN
Lab Zero 5, Florence, Italy

Savio Brudetti, the Creative Director of Lab Zero 5 of Florence Italy, called it "Guerilla V.M." He should know since it was his concept and his company that executed this two day blitz that brought the 1980s and the POP culture of that period to the main square in the university town of Arezzo and to the citizens and the students there.

For one weekend, starting early on a Saturday morning, the Piazza S. Jacopino was alive with music provided by a local DJ — oversized Rubik cubes scattered across the space and a pair of glass enclosed cubes which were "inhabited" by a rotating group of live mannequins. The "cube" with the Pac Man graphics represented the plastic covered boxes that Barbie dolls come packaged in and in this promotion—the live models were "Barbie."

The sponsors of this event or happening, Pulzelli — a large fashion specialty store on the Piazza in Arezzo — not only provided the garments that the assorted Barbies wore who lived and interacted in the cubes in one half hour shifts, they also provided the 5000 real Rubik cubes that were distributed on the square. According to Savio

Brudetti, "The Rubik cube is one of the symbols of these years along with Barbie." Together with the Pac Man symbols that decorated the store windows facing the piazza, they were also applied to the giant cubes on the piazza." These games bring back thoughts of childhood and pleasant memories."

The students of the local University of Urbano were involved with this project from its inception. A week before the break of the Pop Up in the Piazza, students were busy "papering" the town with these symbols and signs of Pac Man and the "ghost" logo of the sponsoring store. They were responsible for promoting the event as well as serving as Barbie, distributing the Rubik cubes and generally providing the excitement and stimulating the visitors to the piazza.

In describing "Guerilla V.M., Savio Brudetti said, "With modern V.M. it doesn't necessarily stop within the shop. It goes out into the square — into the streets — among the people including everybody in the dynamics of the promotion."

Timberland Outdoor Performance Exhibit

Outdoor Retailers Market, Salt Lake City, UT

DESIGN
JGA, Southfield, MI

CHAIRMAN & PROJECT PRINCIPAL
Ken Nisch

CREATIVE DIRECTOR
Gordon Eason

EXHIBIT CONTRACTOR
Exhibit Works, Livonia, MI

INSTALL/DISMANTLE CONTRACTOR
Concept 360, Doylestown, PA

FOR TIMBERLAKE CO., THE GLOBAL CREATIVE SERVICES TEAM
SR. DIRECTOR
Bevan Bloemendaal

PROJECT LEADER & SR. MANAGER
David Curtis

FIXTURING MANAGER
Jean Wood

SR. MANAGER CORPORATE MEETINGS & EVENTS
Stephen King

SR. MANAGER OF VISUAL MERCHANDISING
Amy Tauchert

PHOTOGRAPHY
Mark Steele Photography, Columbus, OH

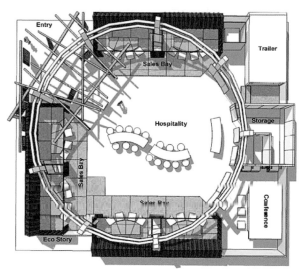

The challenge for JGA's design team was to create a two tier display stand for Timberland that would project the brand and make a definitive statement in the 3000 sq. ft. space at the Outdoors Retailers Winter Market in Salt Lake City. The booth was designed "to reflect the attitudes of a 'new generation' of outdoor consumers, the Millenials. The target consumer's idea of the outdoors is not a passive world, but one of challenges, technology and adventure." JGA had to also show Timberland's "commitment to environmental accountability leveraging its 'nutrition label' concept, incorporating repurposed objects, maximizing operational flexibility, while minimizing negative environmental impact,"

Throughout, the designers conveyed the company's eco-friendly message through the use of recycled industrial objects and natural materials. Shipping containers were repurposed for ongoing shipping and storage and also as booth "room" settings. "The outside of the booth featured a three dimensional 'nutrition label'—a signature element that is part of the outdoor performance packaging and is translated into a large panel element—highlighting the various materials and an environmental 'score card' for full transparency and accountability."

The corner entrance to the booth interior featured a series of overscaled "chop sticks" that created "a tumbled weave" effect that can be rearranged for future shows but served as a filter at this one. The reception desk was located here along with a series of panels that accommodated the display of products and wrappings. The central area of the space served as "a community gathering area" with stand-up counters: it was an easy "meet and greet" space. A hospitality element transformed into a stand-up table for beverage service or for buffet lunch service. Hemp fabric panels

and translucent panels were used to separate an enclosed conference area from the rest of the activities going on. Through the shadows and silhouettes there was a hint of the activity going on inside. A merchandising trailer was "docked" into the booth with its signature crow's nest and a fully fitted-out interior selling space. A six inch elevation of the selling deck created "a physical and visual separation from the social, common area of the booth." A galvanized handrail and the attached marketing panels further delineated the border. There were custom display tables, made of natural materials, with flexible surfaces that enhanced the viewing angle of the product shown on the wall while providing a work surface for the customer. Translucent acrylic panels provided the feeling of natural lighting set as joints between the booth's modules and as vertical skylight elements.

In addition to being selected as Best of Booth at that show, the design was acclaimed for its use of eco-friendly materials that included Marmoleum (biodegradable flooring material), Valchromat wood (produced from pine wood scraps and without formaldehyde), Parallan (material ordinarily wasted in the milling of lumber), hemp (a natural fiber), Echo Eliminator (recyclable sound absorbing material), Flakeboard (from strands of trembling aspen), cork (a renewable material harvested without cutting down trees), and aluminum (recyclable, reusable material sourced from mainly resourced aluminum).

Tital Exhibit
Traveling Exhibit, India

DESIGN
Collaborative Architecture, Mumbai/Calcutta, India

PRINCIPALS
Lalita Tharani, Mujib Ahmed

DESIGN TEAM
Shoukath, Sandhya Banjan

PHOTOGRAPHY
Lalita Tharani

The traveling exhibit designed by Collaborative Architects of Mumbai & Calicut was conceived to fill an exhibit area of about 1500 sq.ft. According to the lead designers on this project, Lalita Tharani and Mujib Ahmed, the client, Titan Industries — a well known brand in India—requested an exhibit pavilion (stand or booth) "which would convey the future directions of the company and at the same time showcase the different brands of the company under one umbrella."

The designers created "individual kiosks for the different brands—with an entire narrative, which takes the spectator through the event (trade show)— unraveling the motto, innovations and the future directions of Titan Industries." "The pavilion is designed to maximize the interface between the audience and the products, prodding the participants to be part of the entire narrative as the pavilion unfolds before them."

The modular display items vary in height and width and can be arranged in a variety of combinations. "The modular units can be arranged to have a number of configurations to fit to the space available and can expand or contract depending upon the site situations." The "feature window" or shadow box opening in each unit is at eye level for ease of viewing the jewelry, watches and such. They "create varied visual stimuli and display sequence — avoiding the generic 'art gallery' effect." Expandability and adaptability were two of the issues addressed by the designers.

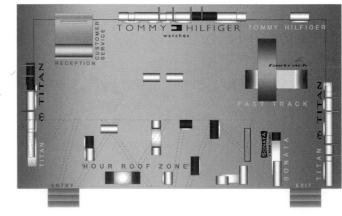

The Mannequin and the Brand

Will Shakespeare knew a lot but back in the 16th century when he asked "What's in a name" he just didn't get it. The "name" is "the brand" and often it is the brand that helps sell the idea or the product. In the early part of the 20th century Gertrude Stein did get it when she poet-isized "a rose is a rose is a rose" because a rose is a rose and has a name and a brand. Today, in the 21st century, we are more visual than in Will's time and though more people are literate—to a degree—and can read but often won't—they respond more readily to visual images like the graphic lettering used to spell out a name or the decorative logo that substitutes for the name.

The students that are majoring in Merchandise Presentation and Exhibit design at the Fashion Institute of Technology (FIT) in NYC were challenged by their faculty—Anne Kong and Mary Costantini—to create "Mannequins Speak the Brand"—using mannequins as a branding tool. Five international mannequin houses provided the mannequins for the students to work on; Ralph Pucci International, DK Display, Manex France Display, Patina V, and Universal Display. To make the challenge even more challenging and focused, the students were restricted to using only paper products and employ pop-up book style applications on the mannequins. It was Paper Sculpture lives again!

In preparation for the assignment, the students went to an exhibition at NYC's Museum of Art & Design (MAD). "SLASH Paper Under the Knife" was the exhibit and the 3rd in a series of "Materials & Processes" at MAD. This time the focus was on paper and unusual treatments of paper in contemporary art and design. The exhibit surveyed the unique paper treatments which included works that were burned, torn, cut by laser or shredded. "The artists in the exhibition do not just see paper as a work surface. They've considered paper's inherent properties and devised ways of transforming this ubiquitous material into extraordinary sculptures, room-sized installations and animations. I think our visitors will be surprised and delighted by what can be done with paper," said Holly Hotchner, the Nanette L. Laitman

Director of the MAD Museum.

The students worked in teams of two and had not only to select the brand and how to "visualize" the brand and interpret it with a costume made of paper, paper products and pop-up or sculptural techniques—but select the mannequin they thought would best represent the brand they selected.

On these pages you will see some of the fabulous dimensional results made by the students. Our congratulations to the students for their clever, imaginative and truly creative brand interpretations, and to the faculty members who guided them along—Mary Costantini and Anne Kong-- for their inspired and inspiring leadership.

Macy's

Herald Square, New York, NY

A Wonder of the World @ Macy's

Fashions change, buildings erode and "good times" come and go but it seems as if Macy's annual Flower Show goes on and on with infinite spellbinding sights, smells and so much more.

This yearly event—now in its 35th year—is a year long project that culminates in March, fresh and in full bloom. We are pleased to show here scenes of the 34th Flower Show—"a blossoming example of the dynamic combination between natural and man-made floral constructions that transform the world's largest store into a vast and vibrant landscape of unparalleled beauty and splendor."

For two weeks in March, Macy's becomes "the largest garden in existence" with the Broadway windows and the entire street level of the store transformed. There were eleven specialty gardens on the main floor including; "Royal Purple," "Cherry Hill," "Miniatures" and "Spanish Gardens."

The always beautiful and exciting windows, created and executed under the imaginative direction of Paul Olsziewski, Director of Windows Visual Presentation, present a glimpse at changing fashions as seen through the ages and the stages of the 20th century. The visual floral bedecked voyage

starts with a Marie Antoinette of the late 18th century in her rose smothered hooped skirt and towering pink cotton candy coiffeur standing in a royal garden full of blooming flowers. The following windows also featured flower dressed mannequins in garments reminiscent of various periods such as the Roaring 20s, the Chic and Shapely 50s—the Mod Days of the 60s—the Disco-fied 70s and the Glamorous 80s. The final floral tribute was to the future—and the fashions it may bring.

Paul Olszewski said, "Since this year's theme is 'a wonder of the world' and Macy's windows are about fashion, I thought it would be fun to combine the two and at the same time, poke some gentle fun at the changing nature of fashion. The Seven Wonders of Fashion windows show how culture and society have shaped what we wear, but at the same time captures the over-the-top nature of both fashion trends and the Macy's Flower Show."

Here's to Macy's and their annual gift bouquet to New Yorkers and all the flower lovers who come each year to behold the blooming miracle.

Macy's

Union Square, San Francisco, CA

SR. VP OF VISUAL MERCHANDISING
James Bellante

VP SPECIAL PROJECTS
Jary Porter

VP CREATIVE SERVICES
Laura Kilpatrick

PHOTOGRAPHER
Doug Diehl, Idealprints.com

Mosaic of Spain @ Macy's

For two weeks during its 62nd annual flower show, Macy's San Francisco celebrated the art, architecture, history, regional cuisine, music—and magic—that is Spain. This was done amid lush greens, thousands of blooming plants and groves of lemon, orange and olive trees.

Visitors were invited to "experience a mosaic of the country's breathtaking beauty and culture," and to sample castles of Castile, the landscapes of La Mancha and thrill to the capricious architecture of Barcelona and the art of Gaudi. In addition to the windows facing the trafficked streets of Union Square, there were vignettes throughout the store to highlight distinct regions and cultures:bullrings, cathedrals, castles, cafes, museums, metropolises, villages and beaches. Then there were the gardens—from Moorish inspired Persian gardens, to lush settings of fruit trees, to expanses of flowering plants.

A shopper entering into the women's store on Geary Street was greeted by a courtyard garden with geranium filled flower pots mounted on the textured walls. Once through the eleven foot high wrought iron gates the shopper stepped into a romantic garden setting with a dramatic fourteen foot tall stone gazebo trimmed with flowering vines. And—as in the gardens of Granada—there was a wealth of blooming wisteria, larkspur and magnolia. Throughout the store the wrought iron gates and columns capped with colorful mosaics in the style of Gaudi were constant reminders of Spain as were the collections of colorful fans and shawls on display.

Brick and stone facades with bougainvillea filled balconies and flower filled terra cotta pots represented a Spanish village at the store's entrance at Stockton and O'Farrell Streets. "The center aisle transported visitors inside the fairy tale Spanish castle to its grand hall, adorned with formal plantings, topiaries, knights in armor" and a magnificent wrought iron chandelier. The Cellar—where Macy's fabulous array of home fashions and foods are usually on show—became a bustling Spanish marketplace aglow with color, patterns and textures and Spanish delicacies to taste and buy.

For the store's windows on Stockton and O'Farrell Streets, the picturesque winding cobblestoned streets of the Barrio Santa Cruz neighborhood were the inspiration for James Bellante, Sr. VPO of Visual Merchandising for Macy's. The barrio is located in Seville and in the windows there were mission bells, a stone wishing well, antique doors and windows and a wooden arbor set amidst succulents, potted and hanging flowering plants and olive and citrus trees. On Geary Street, two ten foot tall decorative pots—weighing over a thousand pounds each—made a big statement while the store's two week message was clearly defined by the gigantic glass mosaic stretched across the façade of the building.

The display field is not so much in need of "rising stars" as it is in need of a firmament in which they can shine. There is lots of talent out there — discovered and not — just waiting for their piece of the retail "sky" in which to burn bright. Lucy Ann Bouwman is another "star" who has twinkled brightly in shadow boxes in prestigious jewelry windows in Boston and Montreal, and is now doing

her shining in the windows of the Hermès and Valentino boutiques in Boston.

We are showing two simple and ingenious promotions she created for Hermès. Using concepts she learned many years ago as a student at Fashion Institute of Technology in New York and polished and perfected over the years, she cleverly turns everyday, ordinary things into eye-

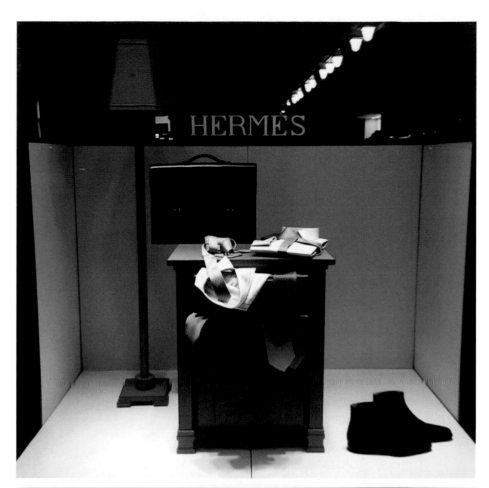

catching and unique display props. The displays shown on these pages show what can be done with small-scale furniture in small, semi-closed windows.

The all-white ambiance features assorted pieces of furniture — all readily borrowed from a local furniture store in exchange for a credit card in the window — or rented for usage. The assorted pieces of Hermès garments and accessories are draped on, in, or spilling out of drawers that are raised up off the floor and closer to the viewer's eye. The rich, natural wood complements the mainly black garments and accessories.

Hermès

Boston, MA

DESIGN
Lucy Ann Bouwman

Do you remember clothespins? I did not think they were still being produced. But, for those of a certain age — before driers in the laundry room — clothespins and clotheslines for drying garments out in the open are a fond memory. Lucy Ann not only collected hundreds of these relics of a bygone era, but created a series of unusual decorative props out of them. Since Hermès is French, Bouwman recreated some French architectural icons with the clothespins and also some sky- and cloud-patterned versions of these icons that she has hung out to dry on the clotheslines.

The same sky/cloud paper appears in panels behind an orange painted "antique" washing machine while an out-of-fashion ironing board (who irons anymore?) serves as an elevation for accessories. In other windows the blue and white print is used to make miniature shopping bags that complement the "bags" covered with clothespins or the bucket enveloped with them. For men's accessories Hermès ties and cloud paper ties are streaming out of a clothespin covered container. Who says that you can't do something new and different with things out of the past?

Le Chateau
Toronto, ON, Canada

DIRECTOR OF DISPLAY
Shawn Schmidt

SR. VISUAL COORDINATOR
Clinton Ridgeway

INSTALLATION & PRODUCTION
Marti Suter, Lucy Song

PHOTOGRAPHER
James Dorion

Le Chateau is a trendy retail operation that not only caters to young women and men but to numerous ethic groups that shop this flagship store in cosmopolitan Toronto. To celebrate Toronto Fashion Week and also salute the diversity of its clientele, Shawn Schmidt, Director of Display, and Clinton Ridgeway, Sr. Visual Display Coordinator, created and installed "Model Behavior."

This display salutes some of the most famous runway models of the last four decades and the mannequins that bear their likenesses. Featured in the window are the mannequins based on Twiggy, British favorite of '70s, Sayoko Yamaguchi (Japanese), Tina Chow (Japanese- German-American), Pat Cleveland and Tyra Banks (African-American), Yasmin Le Bon (British-Iranian), Karen Mulder (Dutch), Agynes Deyn, Erin O'Conner and Catherine Dyer Bailey (British) Coco Rocha (Canadian) and the Americans Dianne Brill and Diane de Witt. Most of these mannequins were originally sculpted and produced since the '70s by noted British mannequin house, Rootstein.

We hope that you will enjoy this tour down memory lane as you try to identify the mannequins. For those of you who can't be bothered — check out the last images where the names have been superimposed over the mannequins. Have fun!

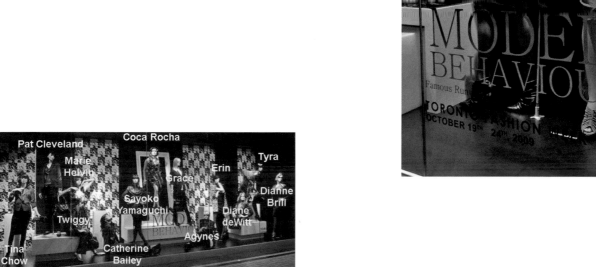

Magic on
Santa Monica Blvd.

Though we usually present displays that have appeared in department stores or designer boutiques, some of the more creative and interesting displays are still happening in the small, independent shops where "magic" happens. The "magic" happens when a retailer who appreciates and respects what attractive and attracting window displays can do for his or her business joins up with a young-at-heart designer/display person full of ideas. The song says "it takes two to tango" and it takes the two to make the "magic" work. The retailer must be part of the equation but there are still too many retailers who just don't get it!

Several years ago we introduced our readers to a new young talent out in California who was making "magic" with a one-window boutique owner. Since then Keith Dillion has increased his range and client list and now also works for another enlightened retailer who owns two stores—just two miles apart on Santa Monica Blvd. in West Hollywood. The stores, owned by Nir Zilberman, feature designer underwear and swimwear for men and are located in a predominantly gay area. Keith works closely

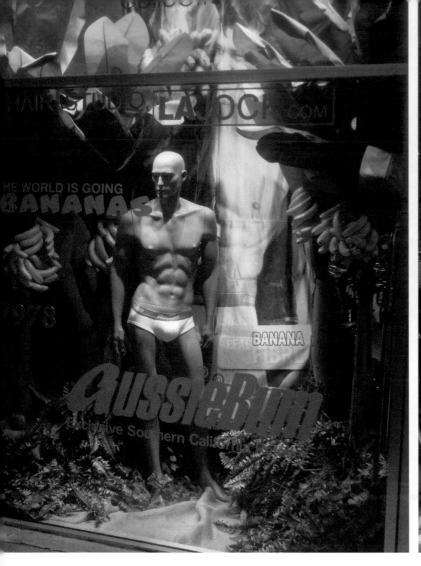

with Nir in planning these displays, and as Keith explains, "The Just One LA themes are usually either seasonal, based around upcoming community events or tropical or beach oriented. Nir loves display and when I meet with him to discuss an upcoming installation, he usually has an idea of what he wants to see based on either the product we will be showcasing or what's going on in the community at that time."

What we find so unique about these displays at Just One LA is that both stores have such relatively small and difficult areas to work in. Both locations feature display areas to either side of the central entrance. In one store the spaces range from 6 ft. wide by 3.5 ft. deep, one side to 3 ft. by 3 ft. on the other. The other store has two areas of 5 ft. by 30 in. These are really cramped spaces where Keith Dillion has to make a big splurge with small garments, life-like mannequins and scene setting props that will catch the eye of the heavy foot traffic on Santa Monica Blvd.

With all these changes—usually every three weeks—we asked Keith how does he manage to be creative working on a budget. He said, "As an artist I see what I could do and what it could be, so the tendency is to go ahead and do those little touches that make it 'perfect' — partly because we all want that all important perfect photo of our amazing creation for our spectacular portfolio, but also because you feel like each person viewing the display will see what it could have been. You cannot always go that extra mile unless the client is willing to cover the cost. Sometimes I will make a calculated purchase that takes me a little — or sometimes a lot — over my budget but this is usually for an item I know that is extremely reusable and could save me on future projects."

In order to come up with ideas and to visualize promotions we asked Keith where he goes for inspiration. His answer was: "Inspiration comes from every imaginable direction. I'm very visual so all sorts of things catch my attention and freeze frame in my mind for later use — people, buildings, architecture, photog-

raphy, artwork, nature. Sometimes, looking at the merchandise, I immediately know how I will approach the display and then my brain pulls together all the necessary information and imagery for me to create it. It's amazing how many times you can see a particular image, prop, mannequin, etc., then, because you are looking at it with a definite purpose — you find a multitude of ideas which were never there before."

He also adds that you must know the target market — whom do you hope to attract with your display and convince to come into the store — and maybe buy the product. "One of the first questions I ask clients is who are their customers. Then I use that information to help develop the look for their displays. Since I specialize in using realistic mannequins, one of the first things I must consider is which mannequins I'm going to use to develop the brand. Just One LA was easy: the customer base is made up of health and image conscious men across a wide age bracket, so I use masculine men with well defined physiques that show off the merchandise to maximum effect with heads that read within that age range. For store that have a more mature clientele, I find that figures with elegant and sophisticated poses and faces which reflect the younger end of their market work best."

Keith Dillion sums it up, "The one common thread is that all of my clients either have a love for display and/or see the impact a great display can have on their business. In turn they appreciate what I do and understand they are paying for what my talent and eye can bring — in the form of attention and sales — to their business."

We are pleased to show you this cavalcade of some recent Just One LA displays from both stores to make the point that lots can be achieved in small spaces when inspiration and talent is there to stretch the space.

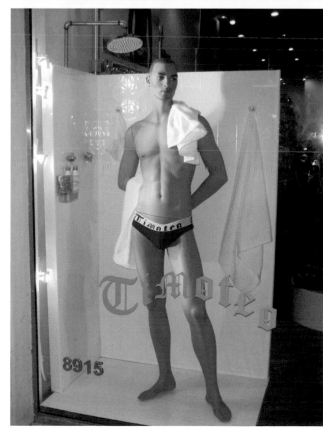

Miss Jackson

Tulsa, OK

VISUAL DIRECTOR
Stacy Suvino

VISUAL ARTIST
Rachel Kern

MEET STACY SUVINO

Stacy Suvino is a winner! Not all that many years ago she was one of the winners in the PAVE (Professionals for the Advancement of Visual Education) contest for college students. At that time she was a student at the Fashion Institute of Technology (FIT) in NYC in the Display & Exhibit department. The design challenge had her pitted against interior design and architectural students from across the U.S. and she came out a winner. And—only last year, PAVE again recognized Su-

vino, this time as one of the "rising stars" of the visual industry. In the four or five years in between she has gone from a job in Bergdorf Goodman's Interior Design department to working in their window display area under Linda Fargo—and that is where she discovered that her heart, mind and talents all came together. This Arkansas-born woman was drawn to the bright lights of New York by a dance scholarship but it was the program at FIT that kept her in the Big Apple.

A personal favorite of Stacy's is the "bubble wrap" window (above left) where she took "things" from around the studio and the storehouse—including frames—and wrapped them in bubble wrap to create this somewhat mysterious setting for Miss Jackson's summer collection. She carried the concept through several windows with assorted items. Nothing is wasted when you can make a display out of it. Note the couture fashion created out of paper plates (top) or the bouffant skirt constructed out of numerous, assorted size boxes (above right). What a great way to show off small fashion accessories, perfumes, toiletries, etc.

"Telephone" windows are a great example of reuse and repurpose as Stacy recycled old telephone books. In one display she created a ball gown out of strips from the yellow pages while in another window she constructed a telephone out of stretched out and worn telephone cords. "It mimics the pattern in the clutch in the mannequin's hand." A series of actual objects, from the display storehouse, have been decoupaged—pasted over with strips of paper from the phone books. They include classic busts, teacups and saucers, lots of picture frames (Stacy has found numerous ways to reuse and reuse her collection of frames), and a chandelier suspended off of a telephone cord. If you look closely you will see that the couch and table are constructed of out-of-use-but newly reused telephone books.

For one of her holiday themes Stacy took a very personal look at Alice in Wonderland (above). For her version of the Mad Tea Party "the back wall is covered with painted silhouettes of various characters from the book and the 'mad hatter' (the mannequin) is surrounded by decadent desserts and lots of tea cups and saucers—including on the chandelier." She is especially pleased with her "Big Alice" window. Stacy explains, "The window depicts when Alice grows larger than her surroundings. It's very minimal but has lots of impact. The scale of Alice compared to the tiny chandelier hanging over the tiny dining table is humorous."

Always looking for ways to get the shopper's attention and to bring her closer to the window, Stacy created a series of "upside down" windows (opposite). In each case the mannequin stand upright but her surroundings have gone topsy-turvy. The mirror and the sconces are inverted and in another window the floor is the ceiling and the ceiling is the floor. The picture frames make a fresh appearance with the lit chandelier hanging down (actually standing up) from the ceiling that really is the floor.

Though her first job in "display" was at Abercrombie & Fitch, it was her internship at Bergdorf Goodman that convinced her that this was the career for her. School was great but it was at Bergdorf that she took her "advanced course" and "learned about details, how to source, use of tools, how to style, how to strike a mannequin, how to merchandise, how to rig, how to put a complete story together and how to have an editing eye."

Now, at still a young and tender age, she is doing all sorts of wonderful and imaginative things as the Visual Director at Miss Jackson in Tulsa, OK. Miss Jackson is a smart, elegant and upscale shop that caters to a prestigious clientele. At Miss Jackson Stacy is responsible for all the windows and the store interior displays, sourcing and styling the fashion shows, store signage and the visual merchandising. Her fun and whimsical spirit seems to match the store's brand and her displays are often surreal—out of the box—but definitely eye-catching. For the store's 100th birthday, Stacy breathed new life and spirit into her decade-by-decade display of the company's history.

Stacy has been with Miss Jackson for almost three years and she keeps coming up with new, different and often startling windows. She absorbs ideas from all around her, from people such as fashion photographer Tom Walker whose photos she once based a series of windows on, to art, fashion and "something I see on the street." Ideas are all around—you just have to be open to "see" them and interpret them. On these pages are reviews of some of Stacy Suvino's window displays annotated with her comments.

What you see here is "a mix of glamour and simplicity" and a sense of humor. We hope you have enjoyed meeting Stacy Suvino and this sampling of her talents. We look forward to seeing and showing more of her projects from time to time. Meanwhile—we salute this Rising Star—Stacy Suvino.

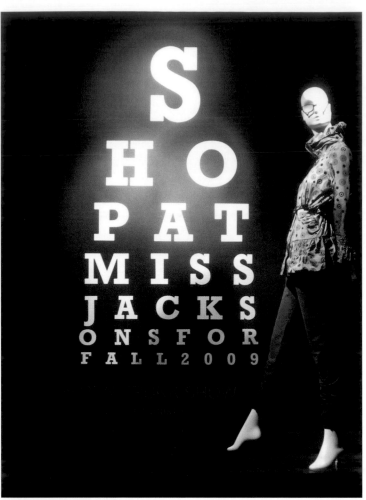

Always one for a laugh—but will settle for a friendly smile—is the series based on "Optometry." A large eye chart actually spells out the promotional message while in another window an all black-and-white fashion setting reiterated the sharp black and white of the eye chart. The last window is one with humor and features a room vignette filled with "patients" and their pets all fitted with eye glasses. Note the return of the frames to help create the waiting room setting.

The Holiday windows for 2009 were inspired by what a circus, circa 1920, may have been like. "One window features a magician who has sawed a girl in half in front of an awestruck audience. Another window is an ornate circus wagon painted and gold-leafed and encases two glamorous mannequins. Another is a ringmaster with a top hat made of 'hair.' She is surrounded by carnival letters that spell out 'big top' and the wall is covered with old circus posters. The final window shows a series of performers including a tightrope walker. This window has a very editorial feel with the mix of glamour and simplicity."

A Fine Italian Hand

Martin M. Pegler

This is not meant to be chauvinistic or a put-down: this is meant as a compliment. There is a familiar expression about "a fine Italian hand" that has two meanings. Not so nice is that it suggests Machiavellian craftiness, but in a much more complimentary way, it refers back to when the work of the medieval manuscript writers was compared to the exquisite handwriting of the Italian scribes. What has that got to do with us?

I recently took a trip to Italy and, rather than doing the tourist-must-see route of Rome, Florence and Venice, I visited Bologna, Ferrara, Ravenna, Parma, Como, Bellagio and Bergamo. Most of these cities are noted not for fashion but for their foods — pastas, sauces, cheeses, hams, wines — and medieval enclosed enclaves, forts and palaces and wonderfully kept "old towns," However, as you walk the crooked, cobblestone paved lanes of these old

towns — where the buildings are so close together and a single auto can barely eke through — you find that the street level of these ancient buildings have been converted into shops selling smart and sophisticated merchandise. This is where the "fine Italian hand" comes in!

I just couldn't resist taking pictures of the store windows where everything looked so delectable. Not big on props nor scene-setting decoratives, these are mostly "mom'n'pop" shops or "designer" boutiques — though you wouldn't recognize the designer's name. Not all the shops are great but many are wonderful to behold. For one thing the amount of merchandise in the window is limited. Not everything is on display — only the newest and the choicest and the most representative items make it into the window. And although energy is costly (some stores still have timers and lights go on in the store when the door is

opened), the windows are beautifully illuminated way past closing time. Proof? All of these pictures were taken with a point and shoot digital camera with the flash off — and no tripod! So, what you see is what I saw and the colors are true. And most importantly, the merchandise was pressed, pampered and pleated — plaids matched, stripes were straight, no threads dangled from hems, and what was soft and draped appears in soft, natural folds. No fabric was made to do what it wasn't meant to do. Since layering and the like, through and through look so "in," each garment was presented to the target shopper in an easy, relaxed manner. This is where the "fine Italian hand" comes in — it knows its fabrics and allow them to fall — take shape and drape as they were meant to.

Interestingly, contrary to the trend in the U.S. towards using abstract and semi-abstract mannequins, here realistic mannequins are the mannequins of choice. I admit that for years I have been collecting "horror" mannequins: mannequins allowed to stay too long in the window — to melt or molt — to sag— to decay — to all but wither and die from exposure to the sun and the elements. I saw very few here. One was used to "model" wares in a flea market outside a palace in Ferrara. These gals and guys that made it into the windows were mainly carefully tended to and treated with respect. Not only were they well dressed, they were in A-1 condition. Also — most of the stores had open backed windows with a clear view into the shop. The

shops were something else! I am a great fan of reuse/repurpose and recycle and get turned on seeing old things used in new ways, so imagine my delight with old stone or chevron patterned worn brick floors, whitewashed stuccoed walls and either ancient, blackened timber ceilings or a fantasy of arches and grains in vaulted ceilings that were testaments to these centuries old buildings. Yet with all those "wonders" the single or trio of figures were so effective and dynamic in the limited spaces that my eyes never went past the presentation on display.

I have no attempt to either identify the shops or the towns where these pictures were taken. Let it suffice that these are "tipico" — these were the norm and the expected. The shops were mainly in Bologna, Bellagio, Bergamo and Como — though I may have shot a few along the way. It is the care, the respect and the evident preparation that went into getting these garments ready for exposure and a tribute to the presenters for how they handled the garments and allowed the garments to "speak" for themselves. I don't think you have to be Italian to have a "fine Italian hand" but from what I saw it helped, and it helped that the neighboring stores and the stores down the long, narrow, twisting streets had shopkeepers who also had "fine Italian hands" working for them.

I wonder if Berlitz or any other of the "learn-a-language-in-three-weeks" school has a course in "Fine Italian Hand on Fabrics?"

WHAT IS VISUAL MERCHANDISING?
THE EXPERTS SPEAK

Many years ago I heard a speaker say something that I have since adopted as my own and often refer to in my own little sermons. It is the comparison of the retail store to an iceberg. The Titanic reasoning goes like this. Every good and successful retail operation has to have a firm and solid base which keeps it secure and anchored in the shifting tides of the economy. That base consists of the retailer's business acumen—knowledge of the field—knowledge of the suppliers—the target market and his ability to buy the best products at the best price—and then sell them at the fairest prices. The retailer must know how to establish himself in the community—in the market—be able to tie-in with his shoppers and have the kind of service and service-pro-

viders that help to make a store's reputation. It means trained sales people, good relations with the shoppers and a follow through or continued relation with the customer after the sale has been made.

BUT—all of these factors—necessary to the store's success lie beneath the waterline and are not visible to the shopper. What the shopper sees is what rises up above the water line. Some—who don't know better—say that it's just so much decoration and frou-frou. However—what the shopper actually sees and what makes the first and often lasting impression of that store is all based on the design, the decor and the ambiance of the retail space.

The store's windows are the official greeters and they are part of the tip of the iceberg. They make the first impression. They not only show the range and quality of the merchandise within but—by how they are present-

ed—they create the store's look—image—appeal. The windows should reach out and envelop the shopper and draw her in. They should show some sense of class and style and indicate the type of shopper who would want to shop here. Inside—that first impression is either reinforced and solidified—or it all sinks. The temperature in the store matters! The light levels and how the light is distributed matters. The kind of light that is used matters. The color and general overall tone of the space matters. The true test comes when the shopper goes looking for what she came in for. Is there a helpful person there to assist? Are there clear and understandable signs? Directionals? Graphics that show and help to sell? Visual aids and displays? How does the shopper know where anything is?

Once she finds the line-up of coffee makers or toasters or cashmere sweaters—how does she know which is which and what does what and goes with what? Are

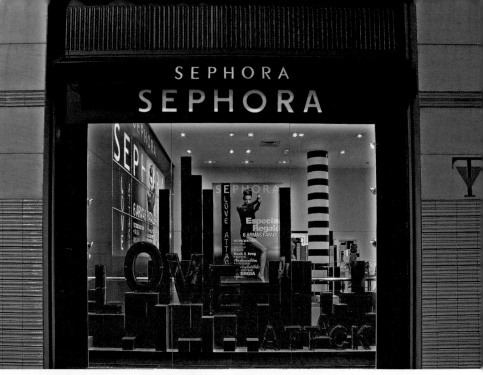

there eye-tempting displays that "show & sell"? Are there counter top set-ups that create the "ideal kitchen"—or a table top all set out for a dinner party or for an informal buffet—or day-in-the-country outfit complete with color coordinated "go-with" and "go-together" products brought together from all over the store to create an attractive, impulse-shopping experience? Are we providing a store filled with "oh's" and "ah's" and "I must have" products? This is where the shopper makes her buying decision.

Maybe it is all sugar coating and pink icing on this tip of the iceberg but it is what the shopper sees—that excites her—stimulates her and makes her want to buy. All of this "eye-candy" is the visual merchandising and display that makes it easier for the shopper to see—to select—to put together—and to buy. AND YES!! Good

salesmanship, knowledgeable help, welcoming and courteous behavior also are visibly part of the retail iceberg tip. It is here that the company's policies and purchasing acumen are tested and proven.

SO—how exactly do we define that appeal to sight? Is that VM? Is it display? Is it merchandising or presentation—or both? We have asked some architects, store designers, interior designers and visual presentation specialists to provide us with their definition of "Visual Merchandising."

(Continues on following page)

Ken Nisch, Chairman of JGA and noted designer
(see Timberland Exhibit page 180) on Visual Merchandising:

"I think that there is a distinction between visual merchandising and displays. I would consider displays being areas such as seasonal décor; areas that are not delegated for customer shopping, but primarily used to show goods being used for their vision and purpose (going to a party, entertaining, organized around a room in the house), or with the pure intention of prompting an emotional reaction.

Visual merchandising, on the other hand, takes into account ease of shopping, creating a coordinated arrangement that considers account space efficiency, productivity of space; the texture, scale and design of a product (while maintaining the shopability and productivity), integrating signage, product information, pricing, and doing so in a way that it can be replicated and maintained within the realities of the consumer and retail environment.

There are those rare cases where companies, who because of the focus that they put on both of these aspects—Crate and Barrel, Anthropology and Whole Foods—where they bring both together, but it is quite a rarefied world. There are also examples such as Target, who I would say never executes a "display" but focuses primarily on the standards of visual merchandising. Also note compa-

nies such as Bergdorf's, who do not practice visual merchandising, but rather, purely displays.

Yes, I do believe that both titles are relevant. They are distinctive and the retailers that use one, the other, or both, are as well, distinctive."

David Dalziel, a principal at Dalziel and Pow Design Consultants of London (Wrangler page 78 and Magic Attic page 104) had this to say:

What is VM?

VM has replaced the long established discipline of Store Display and has now increased it's relevance to us in the creation of the Total Brand Environment. We need to be aware of trends in this area and Design Concepts that integrate these trends or work with inspired clients who include these skills in-house.

In-House Display teams have been replaced by Creative Brand Directors and they have become one of the Design Team, stretching from the display of product into the manifestation of the Brand in it's entirety, often touching on Brand Communications in-store.

APPROPRIATE VM...

Increasingly the clients we deal with are keen to recognise the role of VM, but equally keen to control the cost and scale of installations The VM budget might now fall under Marketing rather than Operations of Store Development and that Marketing budget needs to be part of a bigger plan. Increasingly the retailer is realising that they can re-direct a conventional Advertising budget into In-Store VM and make a bigger statement for the Store and their customers. Appropriate solutions are not always constrained by cost, occasionally it is appropriate to invest heavily to create that Wow factor so rare in today's retail.

EXTERIOR VM...

The Exterior architecture of a store has never been more crucial in presenting a Brand approach and inspiring shoppers to shop. In the recent launch of Westfield London, 200 stores presented their latest and best ideas and some excelled in the embracing of VM as a definition of their Brand.

INTEGRATED VM...

The definition of VM and Store Design is now blurred with the better stores integrating their Display concepts into the overall store environment. Whether seasonal or Brand driven these hot-spots in store are no longer occasional or isolated but fundamental to the success of the overall look and feel."

Wolfgang Gruschwitz of
Gruschwitz Retail of Munich
sees VM this way:

"Today, visual selling exceeds mere decoration to a large extend. An interaction of
light, fragrance, images and other messages creates a temporary statement at the
POS, to seduce the costumer and to make him or her decide in favour of a purchase. To create needs, to attract the customers to each shopping area and to make
them touch the goods set into scene, to anchor the brand within the customer's
mind and to appeal to the respective attitude of life—all this is covered by the func-
tion of a today's Visual Merchandiser. The Visual Merchandiser is the person, who
vitalizes the brand at the POS and who fills it with life for the customer."

Michael Malone, architect and designer and principal at Michael Malone Studio (M Penner on page 66) sums VM up this way:

"In our world Good Visual Merchandising is what our clients do within the framework of the stores and fixtures we design. When we first interview for a new retail design project it is often the first time I see a potential client's present store environment. Even if the design of the store is old or dated, you can still discern whether or not they value the way their merchandise is presented and organized, how they feel about propos and visual elements, their use of lighting and often most important, their commitment to housekeeping.

I have worked with successful retailers who have terrible retail environments in which to sell, but who use what they have in a clever and thoughtful manner, combined with their good taste and careful buying to create exceptionally successful retail presentations. Conversely I have clients for whom we (or others) have designed beautiful stores, but who have no commitment to visual merchandising and their goods look flat and thoughtlessly presented, despite the exceptional opportunities their stores offer.

My own personal design style lends itself to the minimal in both design elements and finishes. In the hands of a talented visual merchandiser or merchant, these environments become contributing backdrops to beautiful stories about the things for sale and the potential for gratification owning them provides."

And—for a completely different angle, we have this "definition" from **Paul Olszewski,** Director of Windows at Macy's New York City.

"I would define visual merchandising (or presentation) as the process of using design principles to sell merchandise. The basics elements of design (color, balance, rhythm, scale, balance) all come into play in good visual merchandising, but always to focus the customer's attention on the merchandise. Visual Merchandisers both educate and entertain the customers, but never lose focus on the product. In window presentations, visual merchandising can be theatrical, whimsical, straight forward or technologically advanced. The purpose is always still to sell, but by catching the eye to draw the customer into the store."

For more and more varied explanations of this wide and wonderful field of Visual Merchandising—keep tuned for our next issue with more definitions from the world of talent.

INDEX